Praise for Carolyn North

"Wow, Carolyn dear, what a powerful piece of writing. I feel you through my heart, soul and body. You are amazing and to me, living proof of the power of the resiliency and shining gift of the human spirit."

> —Shilpa Jain, Executive Director of YES! WORLD

"Oh Carolyn, this is transcendent. You yourself are the music while the music lasts. Thank you for putting this all into words."

> —Mary Felstiner, Professor Emeritus, University of San Francisco

"I think an angel sits somewhere in your psyche and laughs at this whole dreadful mess and says see I told you—she is the most amazing of the daughters of life. Wow. Just wow."

> —Cynthia Winton Henry, Co-founder of Interplay, Global Social Movement About Unlocking the Wisdom of the Body

"Carolyn's words continue to be an active roto rooter to help dislodge thought forms that get mired in the bogs of futility and cynicism. I'm grateful they are finding a way to hit the airwaves and reach more people and am honored to blow some wind into the sails of her writings."

> —Lauren Brown

Other Books by Carolyn North

The Musicians and the Servants: A Novel of India

Seven Movements, One Song: Memoir as Metaphor

The Experience of a Lifetime: Living Fully, Dying Consciously

Ecstatic Relations: A Memoir of Love

Serious Fun: Ingenious Improvisations on Money, Food, Waste and Water, & Home (to which *WorldShift Happens!* is a sequel)

WorldShift Happens! Facing Down the Fear, Waking up the Mind

Voices Out of Stone: Magic and Mystery in Megalithic Brittany (with Natasha Hoffman)

In the Beginning: Creation Myths from Around the World (with Adrienne Robinson)

The Fringe Series

Crop Circles: Hoax or Happening?

Synchronicity: The Anatomy of Coincidence

Death: The Experience of a Lifetime

Musings on the Passing Scene: 2011–2014

The Living Edge of Dying: Musings in an Era of Breakdown: 2015–2017

Closer to the Bone: Musings in an Era of Change: 2017–2018

Freeflow Stories

Musings on
the Passing Scene:
2018–2022

ICRL Press
Ewing, New Jersey

Listen to the serialized audiobook version of Freeflow Stories (and other books by Carolyn North) on the podcast, Carolyn North Out Loud. Stories are read for you by the author and others, including the actress Amy Walker and the show's producer, Leslie Jackson.

All episodes: www.carolynnorthbooks.com and wherever you get your podcasts.

Freeflow Stories
Copyright © 2022 by Carolyn North
ISBN: 978-1-936033-39-3

Cover design by Sara Glaser
Book design by Leslie Jackson
Lotus illustration by Georgianna Greenwood

Address all correspondence to:
ICRL Press
P.O. Box 113
Sykesville, MD 21784

Freeflow Stories is dedicated to the memory of Brenda Dunne—partner for decades in playful witchery and serious fun—who happened to pass on precisely when this dedication was being written. But that was the way of our game!

Farewell, dear Witch of the East; I shall miss you.

Table of Contents

Introduction

I have been writing these little stories every two weeks for almost 12 years now, sending them out to friends and anyone interested in receiving them, thanks to the magic of e-mail.

My rules for myself have been that each story be the length of a newspaper column, and deal lightly with some of the hard issues of our time through telling my own dilemmas of the moment. I wanted to make you smile with recognition, and to offer a positive spin on some of the difficult realities we are all facing. I wanted for my little stories to say, "we can do this, folks!"

I wanted to point to a way of seeing our world as somehow larger—much larger—than we have been taught to view it. I wrote them to encompass the unseen, the inexplicable, the so-called 'impossible.' I wanted to love what I love and to say why I did; I wanted to rail against harm and injustice all the ways I saw it. I wished to point out a deeper level of reality than is commonly understood in our culture, and to do so without apology.

In other words, I wanted to go deep and include the expanded parameters of science and spirituality to our daily lives and to recognize that every single one of us—no matter how or where we live—belongs in it.

The first of these pieces simply came to me on a BART train one night after seeing a dance performance of the Alonzo King LINES Ballet Company. I was still in thrall from the fabulous performance of those dancers, and this sentence simply popped up unbidden in my mind like a kind of *cri de coeur:*

"I want to dance the way Black men do!"

Of course I am a little nonplussed by my old dream, but I would still love to be able to do what they can do—fly through the air and land on my feet softly; leap and be caught in mid-air; sink and rise like a swift dolphin in the waves! There on the rushing train, sentences rose into my mind and demanded to be caught before I forgot them … it was a good thing I had a pen in my purse, and the Playbill to write on as we sped through the tunnel, because that first piece came pouring out of me like freely flowing water. And these little pieces were born.

For a dozen years these small pieces have been emerging from my life every two weeks like clockwork through a historic time in the world, through environmental disasters and stolen presidencies, through the polarizing era of Trump and an ongoing pandemic involving every person on the planet!

And the death of my beloved husband after 57 years of our marriage.

But these years have also been witness to a growing tide of new thinking and the growing awareness of the wisdom of the heart, and the fact that we are in the midst of a huge planetary shift of consciousness as we make a wide turn the way an ocean liner might change direction in mid-ocean, setting its sight for a different shore.

It has not always been easy to find the silver linings in these stories, but it has been my task to watch out for them—and indeed, I find them! I discover them hiding right there, in you and me and everywhere, hidden in plain sight.

Just look—I expect you'll find them too. I trust these stories will find their way to those who need to see and hear them as we go through this scary, but amazing time in the world!

So here you have it—my ordinary life, my sense of humor and my understanding of this time in the world—served up in bite-sized pieces like chocolate-covered cherries where your tongue tastes the tart fruit right before you swallow the sweet liquor. I have chosen and collected these stories for a small book that you can hold in your hands, and curl up with cozily beneath a quilt when the winds are blowing outside, in quarantine or not; alone with your thoughts or cozy with friends and family.

I sincerely hope these stories help us make it through with our senses of humor intact, as it has certainly helped me to write them!

Thanks to Brenda Dunne from ICRL, the International Consciousness Research Labs in Princeton, for suggesting I collect these pieces for a book, after spending many a glad hour on the orange couch in the basement PEAR office with a teddy-bear on my lap, hashing out ideas about the evolution of consciousness. A huge bow to Leslie Jackson who simply knew so brilliantly how to create a book from scratch when it became necessary to do so. It has been an honor and a pleasure to work with you, dear Elf. To Brighid Fitzgibbon for that gorgeous waterfall photo on the front cover, to Alexandro Strauss for the gorgeous waterfall photo on the back cover, and to Sara Glaser for designing the cover.

Finally, I bow to the choreographer Alonzo King who, whether he knows it or not, started this whole project years ago through his dazzling company of dancers in the LINES Ballet Company, and the visionary works he continues to create for them from his unquenchable imagination.

The first story, I've Always Wanted To Be A Black Male Dancer, is for you, Alonzo!

Carolyn North
Wild and Radish Farm,
El Sobrante, California
June 17, 2022

11

I've Always Wanted To Be
a Black Male Dancer

For as long as I can remember, my dearest wish has been to be a Black, male dancer. My first serious dance teacher, in the 1950s, was Donald McKayle, a tall, dark Appollo from somewhere in the Caribbean, I think, and my ideal has forever since taken his form. Never mind that I am female, indisputably Caucasian and currently too old to perform on a stage, but still, after tonight's performance of the LINES Ballet company in San Francisco, the old longing came back powerfully. Glorious as the whole company is, it was those men, unhampered by toe shoes and chiffon, bursting strong and free onto the stage, that brought back all those impossible early yearnings of the young dancer I once was.

This morning, musing in bed, I can still feel their moves in my body as those guys arose out of the wings with wings, and danced the dance of life in all its creative possibility. I saw their power and their poignant subtlety, their consummate skill and their freedom. They were beyond beautiful to me—they were life itself, the life I wish to live and the beauty I wish to bring to the world. In human form they were the metaphor and model I want to embody, and the energy of the words I try, as a writer, to write.

Here is what they evoke for me: the discipline and skill that gives them their freedom to fly; I want to live as they dance, with 100% of myself, taking risks from the balanced safety of my whole being. I wish to rise high in the air and leap, as they do, extending myself to the limits of my body. I want to have no doubts about my abilities, knowing that even at rest I am gorgeous, as they are, and in motion know how to take ever-changing shapes that express the wildness and subtlety of my being. I want my every breath to count, and my heart to beat with the rhythm of the music so that I can convey in every move the beauty of the world, as they do. That's the kind of artist—the kind of person—I want to be every day.

Those metaphors lit for me up in the balcony where I watched in thrall the range of their genius, their moving shapes, their quiet stillness. Their spines were supple and strong enough to carry each other, and their muscles relaxed enough to be carried; they made seemingly impossible leaps of faith, landing where trust in each other had to be perfect. They took solos and shone, and then they provided backup for the shining of the others. With grace they assisted one another, gave space and support and found their unique places in the design of the whole. Their bodies sang with the great fun they were having, unfettered, self-assured and powered by the innate creativity of the universe. I was so jealous! Not only did I long to be able to do what they did, but I wanted to *be* them!

I cannot be them—never could, probably. But here's what I think I *can* do: I can watch them dance and imbibe the quality of their dancing into my own being. I can be grateful that they exist in the world for us in the audience to experience; I can know that if a small troupe of dancers can, with discipline, talent and the desire to do so, create such magical beauty, then the world is capable of surviving our times despite so much evidence to the contrary. I can feel assurance, even in my bleakest moments, that dancers and artists and writers like these can inspire those who come after me to also create a vision of what excellence looks and feels like, and that everything I live for will not be lost when I am gone.

But. Still.

Might I, please, if there is such a thing as a next life after this, can I please come back as a male dancer? With a dark-skinned body, if possible?

Home Sick

I'm someone who enjoys the occasional bad cold, when I get to drop all my to-dos and lie back for a few days of self-indulgent misery. Tucked in bed with hot drinks, warm socks and the phone turned off, I choose some well-loved novel I've read at least once before and disappear into its delicious familiarity, getting reacquainted with its people and places and hearing the story anew from my life here and now.

This time I am reading Rosamund Pilcher's *The Shell Seekers* which takes place mostly in Cornwall, England where I have long ago had winter adventures and summer ones, been in love and walked those cobbled streets. I know the sea there, and the light, and how it smells with coal fires burning in winter, and the feel of misty rain soaking into my anorak.

I lay back now and slow down to a daydream of times gone by and feelings long forgotten. I remember …

The cows, a whole herd of them surrounding me in a pasture where I have gone, all alone in winter, to check out some standing stones outlined upon the hill. The cows have followed, curious, and stand around me in a loose circle, huffing smoky breaths into the cold air.

Up close, cows are huge beasts and I wonder if I should be worried about being trampled. They gaze at me with enormous brown eyes and eyelashes that curl beguilingly, so I tell them why I'm there in their field, and I ask them what they know about these stones I am leaning against. I explain why I have come, in my most soothing voice, and wonder out loud how I am going to escape when it is time.

They have all the patience in the world and seem un-inclined to move, so, having run out of words I start to sing. I make up a riff that grows into a repeated theme and variations. The cows move in closer, their eyes growing soft, and I keep singing, letting the song sing itself on this hillside near Land's End, shifting from major mode to minor, adding syntax in three octaves and playing with whatever sounds evoke a response in the cows. But they only come in closer, their wet noses sniffing me out and their hooves within knee-knocking distance of mine. By this time, I am scared.

The only person I know in all of Cornwall is the boy I have just broken up with, the heavy mist is turning to rain and I am trapped by cows in a field I know not where.

My song grows a bit desperate and turns to a Gospel beat, beseeching the Lord to help me out of this fix. I rock from one foot to the other, as Gospel singers do, and clap out the rhythm with wet hands. The cows are fascinated and they blink, watching my clapping hands, which are of course the 'open sesame,' and then they grow restless and slowly part ranks, turning and lumbering off. I watch them go, astonished, and when the way is clear I beat a retreat back to the road and make my way in the direction of St. Ives.

On another trip, also mid-winter, I am traveling with an English cousin I am visiting, and we decide to each spend the day having solo adventures. Again it is lightly raining, and I take the coastal path up on the cliffs and start out to the west. I've brought neither map nor money nor compass, figuring the path leads only in one direction and there is nothing to buy out there in the wilds anyway. It's just me and the sea and sky, the wind and rain and this ancient landscape holding so many millennia of stories.

During a squall I take shelter beneath a quoit, an ancient structure of massive, balanced stones that have stood here since time immemorial. Who has built this, when and why remains a mystery, but for a bit it keeps the rain off me, holding its secrets intact.

The squall passes, the sun is revealed for a moment and a rainbow appears over the sea as I emerge out from under, and continue down the coastal path towards whatever I will encounter next. Which, after some time of walking, is a tiny greystone village with a Norman church tower and a clutch of cottages and pub around it. The rain has started again and I am truly soaked through, but I have brought no money for a hot drink at the pub. Foolish woman! But I see a fire blazing inside and perhaps they will just let me dry out a bit. I am greeted as soon as I enter,

"Hallo darlin', you are wet!"

"Yes I am," I admit with a small laugh (and my American accent.)

"You are an American?" The publican asks, beckoning me over to the bar, "an American?" He seems charmed and I imagine not too many tourists make it this far down the coastal path, especially in the rain. "Come here my darling, and let me give you something hot to drink. Better, come into the back room and take off your clothes …"

Uh-oh, what have I just walked into?

"The Americans saved my life in the war, and at last I can repay them their kindness," he announces, bustling me into his family quarters, handing me a bathrobe while he gathers my wet clothes and puts them into the dryer to dry. A bowl of hot soup is placed in front of me, a steaming mug of tea and a huge crust of bread. "You just take your time, dearie, while everything dries. Look, it's sleeting now, but you're warm and dry as you should be."

I slurp the thick hot soup, my heart warmed as well as my body with the unexpected wonders of life in this world. I can still taste that broth, the strong tea and the crunch of that *barmbrack* between my teeth. I can hear the thunk of the dryer behind me, and the guys in the pub gathering round the publican as they compare stories of the war—and speculation about me, no doubt. Where am I? How have I gotten here? How did I walk right into a welcoming haven when I set out for high winds and wild waves?

I still had a long walk back, my clothes were dry and hot and the rain had let up, so if I left right away I could make it back to the B&B before dark, but when I appeared at the bar to say 'goodbye' and 'thank you,' I was told,

"No darling, I will take you back in my car."

"But …"

"Do not argue, I would not dream of letting you wander out there on your own. Your people saved my life and the least I can do is to bring one of theirs safely home. Now, I cannot do it until I close the pub at 5, but why don't you stroll around and see our little village. I think they will be practicing ringing the bells in the church. I'll look for you there when I am finished."

Magic. Perfection. Sweetness. The clanging chorus of heavy bells in the nave of the old church, the teenagers lifted into the air as they pull the ropes in rhythm, laughing and swinging, their arms working hard, tones pealing out one after another, shaking my body, heart and soul so that I can still, after all these years, feel them and hear them.

The kindness of strangers; the unexpected magic; the memories that continue to live within you, mostly out of sight in a busy life, but it seems that when you slow way down, as you do when you are home sick, there they are.

Achoo! Ahh-h …

The Joy of Cooking

Alonzo King, the choreographer and founder of LINES Ballet company, told us at an open rehearsal recently that he wanted to work with geniuses. And he does. I know because whenever he opens the rehearsal studio for the public to watch these amazing dancers at work, I go—and they are indeed amazing. He is too. I go not only to see them dance but also to hear him talk about his philosophy of dance and his creative process.

He told us, after someone asked how he choreographs new works, that he listens to what is around and within him, focuses on an impression and then lets it cook. He spoke of letting flavors mingle, of the individual spices that are each of the human beings who dance in his company. He told us that it is a language that communicates something new and unique, and then is served up with love—"an offering of love is what all art is," he told us. "It is a language that nourishes and shares what it means to be human."

Magnificently, in the case of this company, I would add.

I left the studio in thrall as I always do and then, not 24 hours later, reading a book about cooking by Michael Pollan, I found this:

"Cooking is all about connection. It is one of the more beautiful forms generosity takes … but the very best cooking is a form of intimacy. Hand Taste," he writes of the experience of making Kim Chee in Korea, "is the infinitely complex experience of a food that bears the unmistakable signature of the individual who made it … Hand taste is the taste of love."

Don't you love it when the universe lays these perfectly-timed synchronicities at your feet? I do, and when it happens I pay close attention, and this one clearly led me to the kitchen. So Herb and I went out to the garden where the last tomatoes were ripening on the vine, and the crazy cardoon was flinging out new leaves, and collard greens and Peruvian 'ground cherries' and dandelion greens were ready for the picking, so we harvested our dinner. We had no idea what to make with such motley ingredients, but our plan was to get creative and find a way to cook it—just like Alonzo.

"Soak it in olive oil...bring it to a boil..." sang our resident sort-of poet as we sliced the leaves off the cardoon ribs and washed dandelion leaves, chopping and steaming and frying, popping in the tomatoes and ground cherries at the last minute. The kitchen smelled of spice and green, and we tossed the colorful mess over pasta—bitters and sweets, chewy and crunchy all together, fresh from the earth and combined in a brand new way—a first in the history of the world. It's my favorite kind of cooking, simple, unexpected and delicious.

The only recipe is my imagination.

It's also the way I write these little 'columns,' which are designed to communicate both the personal and universal, cook them up in a few pages of words and let them simmer until juicy. Happiness, for me, is getting some unexpected idea and then letting it marinate inside me until it begins to change, calling up memories and feelings that make me laugh or weep. The flavor intensifies until I taste its metaphoric theme and smell its particular aroma; then I know what to do with it and can create a little dish that is new and tasty—doesn't have to be fancy.

Then I serve it up with my love.

This piece started off as a tribute to Alonzo King, but look where it has led, into the kitchen cooking up new stuff! But that's the way good cooking as well as good art happen; you start with some ingredient, give it a little heat, add some of this and some of that and before you know it the ingredients are showing you what they are good for—a braised stew, a crispy salad.

Then you delve deeper into the theme and new possibilities arise. You stir, add some pepper and a touch of turmeric and let it cook some more, tweaking and changing a phrase here and there, adding a swerve of the hip at the last moment and then, by a certain smell in the air you know when it is ready.

Frankly, I cannot think of anything more important for us to be doing right now than cooking up new stuff in new ways with whatever ingredients we have at hand. With governments going bonkers and the economy a runaway train, we've got to get creative in all the small ways, rethinking how to take care of ourselves and each other right close to home, because our survival may depend on it.

It will be hard, but does not need to be dire because hard can also be exhilarating, and the unleashed creative imagination can dream up the most unexpected pleasures—more exciting and delicious than packaged food by a long shot.

We've just got to get into shape, learn how to improvise new moves and combinations and to start practicing. Fine dancers do it; fine cooks do it; fine artists do it.

"And every human being is an artist," Alonzo told us with a smile, "since all art is a language of love."

On Generosity

Twice this week I was rendered speechless by the power of unexpected generosity. The first was an actual gift from someone I barely knew, and the second was a story of survival that took such courage to write that I experienced it as a gift.

The first gift was brought by one of my students, from her mother who I only met once. It was her mother's way of saying thank you to me for loving her daughter so well, and I literally could not speak when I unwrapped it. A weaver, she raises sheep for wool which she shears, cards, cleans, spins and dyes with plant dyes before weaving it into blankets and shawls.

She made a shawl for me, determining my colors from that one time we met—bright autumn shades—and designed it for the person she remembered—me. My hands touched heaven when I unwrapped it, and for several minutes I simply stared, speechless with both the beauty of the shawl and the magnitude of the gift. I imagined the months of work she had done, all the while imagining the person who would receive it. It was as if someone had been praying for me all this time, and me having no idea it was happening.

What goes round, comes round, she might say—reciprocal blessings between two mothers connected by one of their children, and their mutual gratitude for what they each offered. She was thanking me for guiding and loving her daughter—'gathering her to your hearth,' was the way she put it and I, in turn, was grateful for the privilege of teaching such a daughter. And now such a gift!

We were both astounded by one another's generosity.

I am reminded of when I was a student in France, living in a provincial household as a nanny with a wonderful family. All the proprieties were expected of the five children, and therefore of me, including the morning handshakes, the two-cheek kisses and, my favorite of all, the interminable thank-you's that went something like this:

Merci.

Mais c'est moi qui doit vous remercie!

No, it is I who should be thanking you!

No no, it is I who thanks you!

No no no, it is my turn to thank you … and so on. Sometimes it took forever to get out the door! But I know well that feeling of gratitude for generosity, and wanting to give it back. It is built into us, I think, the wish to both honor and be honored, to see and be seen in return, to give and to receive.

This week I finished reading a book for young people, *Gideon* by my old friend, Chester Aaron, a novel about a 14-year-old boy who survived the Warsaw Ghetto. Even though Chester wrote it for children, he pulls no punches and brings us right into an unthinkable world where adults wantonly murder children, parents are rounded up and tortured, and our fellow men—mostly men—become monstrous killing machines obeying orders from shrieking madmen. Very few survive the ongoing slaughter, but some fight back, and this is the fictional story of one who, by his wits and ingenious courage, does—and he lives to tell the tale.

I had to keep reminding myself that Chester himself had not personally experienced the ghetto, although his life was permanently marked by witnessing the carnage, as a young soldier liberating a death camp at the end of the war. That meant that, in order to write this book he had to deliberately bring himself back to his witnessing, as a very young man, the unthinkable world of those who survived.

He had to re-immerse himself in their stories, recall the sights and sounds of unthinkable horror, and then imagine himself a young boy who survived it, who had the courage and wily imagination to stay alive and help others do so, as well.

He wrote this book for himself, I am sure, but he also did it for us.

How long did it take him to write this book, I wonder, all the while living inside the mind of a boy facing unspeakable loss and soul shock amongst fellow humans gone mad? One year, two years?

I am awed by the generosity of my friend, his deliberate choice to spend years of his life bearing witness and reporting back to us through time and space the imagined mind of a 14-year-old boy fighting for his life. In effect he is saying, "You have to know! You have to see the horror and learn from it that yes, humans are capable of unspeakable evil. But you must know that we are also capable of the opposite: of generosity and courage and beauty. Even when we are frightened or in the midst of horror, we are probably stronger than we think. To be human is to be both, and everything in between, and don't you forget it!"

I bow to you both, Rebecca and Chester, with gratitude for your gifts, your generosity, your brilliance and your grace. I wish someday we three could meet.

We would love each other, I'm sure.

Soft Eyes

for Paul Andrews

Over the years, all my writing has been focused on intuitive ways of knowing the world and I use poetic diction and stories to get my point across rather than rational facts. I figure it's through subtlety—'feeling' the way more than 'thinking' the way into knowing—that can help open our hearts as well as our minds to the extraordinary beauty of this amazing Universe we are lucky enough to find ourselves in.

The competition and greed that has been foisted on us by systems based on tough logic, competition and human supremacy is clearly not good for either our species or the planet.

I wonder what it *is* good for.

It happened yesterday that a friend sent me an article about 'soft eyes'—just as I was wondering how to start this piece.

Synchronicity?

"'Soft eyes' is actually an old term used in animal tracking," the article reads, "and is supposedly of Native American origin. 'Soft eyes' refers to the slightly unfocused gaze that takes in the whole field of view at once, all together. 'Hard eyes' see nothing but the object of their focus and are too hard for the world to make an impression on them; information comes from the inside out, from ideas, from pre-conceptions, not from the touch of things. 'Soft eyes' stand back a bit, let the scene unfold—actually see what's there—the multiplicity of worlds, the teem of information, all those planes of existence inter-secting (or not). It's a different kind of knowing."

I love that. Try it. Unfocus your eyes slightly and look softly at whatever is before you. Notice what your peripheral vision sees, and how you 'feel' when you do that. Where in your body do you feel it? Trust that feeling, and foster it for this gives you access to more than what is on the surface of things, and that is when everyday surprises like synchronicities tend to happen!

We call it magic, but this everyday magic is available to every one of us all the time.

Years ago when I was 20 and a new student in a provincial town in France, the father of a friend kindly found me room and board at a nearby Convent, but the very idea chilled my bones. In a quick moment of inspiration, I told him that I was looking for a live-in position as a nanny—an idea that had not crossed my mind until that moment!

Then, wandering the streets, I 'happened' by the University hous-ing office, went in, the woman behind the desk smiled and remarked that she liked my face, and that her neighbor was looking for a nanny from another culture! She made the call, I went right over for tea, had a good connection with both the parents and the children, and two days later I moved into their cozy garret.

I believe I learned more that year from both the synchronicity that got me there, and the de Leffe family I lived with, than from all the courses I took at the University!

Thus began my lifelong study of things 'paranormal.'

Personally, I believe the paranormal—or para-usual, as a friend calls it—is perfectly 'normal' if we extend our awareness to include all the subtle strands of experience and energy that connect us to one another and to everything else in Time and Space and beyond.

In our culture we ignore these levels of experience at our peril, I believe, because if our world is defined as limited, we tend to be vulnerable to control from those seeking power over us. It's an old story and, to say the least, has never been in humanity's best interest. Nor the Earth's.

Just yesterday (by synchronicity, of course) a friend was telling me about her experience years ago at a class for massage therapists, when she 'saw' the skeletal system of the woman she was working on. "It was as if the bones suddenly lit up," she told me, "kind of like an X-ray. I could see how the bones and muscles went together, and my hands just knew where to go." Then she said more quietly, "I shut the vision down quickly, and never mentioned it to anybody because it scared me."

My eyes filled with tears—for her, for us and for myself—because I also often shut down what seems clear to me when I fear that people will think I'm crazy, even though scientists know perfectly well that what we call 'matter' makes up only about 7% of the universe, and they have no idea what makes up the rest.

When I point this out, people tend to shrug.

Surrounded by miracles as we are, if these coincidences don't fit the current paradigm, our shared culture calls them 'wrong' or shrugs and turns away. Even ordinary, everyday synchronicities are considered too woo-woo for the popular media! This at the peril of all of life itself! How arrogant is that?

All I know is that I live with synchronicities on a daily basis and all I know is that I count on these synchronicities to guide me. They fit into my understanding of the world as a multi-dimensional, interconnected and glorious Whole. If everything is connected to everything, and the whole world is in continual motion, then of course these useful intersections are bound to happen, whether or not they make 'rational' sense to our culture's present understanding of how the world works.

Anyhow, whoever called our current life-threatening dilemmas 'rational?' More like 'outrageously insane,' if you ask me!

If you've ever tried to rescue a spider from the shower before you turn on the water, then you know how it scurries wildly from your helping hands. I am reminded of frightened spiders every time I even speak the words 'free energy' out loud in the wrong company, or 'crop circles,' as if my very words had the power to harm. The fact is, however, that free energy devices exist and work without the benefit of fossil fuels, and magnificent artworks have been appearing in fields of grain all over the world by the hundreds for decades—along with some clever hoaxes—and both these phenomena point to solutions for many of our more desperate problems. However, since they point to an expanded understanding of how the natural world works, they are considered somehow unworthy of our attention and worse, even dangerous.

Why? I wonder.

Here we stand at the cusp of either annihilation or an evolving future. The choice is in our human hands linked with every other sentient being in the universe. It would not necessarily be the first time we chose hate over love in our fear of one another and of ourselves, but I so wish we would choose love.

Who knows but that Now—right now—might be our last shot at it.

Why not gird up all our courage and take that shot—essentially learning how to love—despite everything? Sheltering in place gives us a chance to go inside and take a good look at our deep-seated fears, however hard that is. It is to our peril that we not even try.

After all, if synchronicities and magical breakthroughs seem to violate natural law, might it be possible that our problems lie not with the laws of nature themselves, but with our own lack of understanding them?

That gives me chills, but it makes a certain sense, no?

Light on Shadow

for A.R. and T.L.

With the new administration bringing up the problem of our collective 'shadow,' some friends and I have been asking ourselves about our own shadows, recognizing that our personal issues tend to be true for the society as well. These are not necessarily easy conversations, to be sure, but when we can emotionally handle them without backing away, I find their candor and passion exhilarating!

One, a longtime friend and colleague, asked me the other day if I had any idea what it was *really* like to be a Black woman in our society. The fact is that I do not, however much I might think I do, so she spelled it out for me—about being both a woman and a Black person—revealing her raw pain in one horrific story after another.

"You mean you didn't know that was *in the law?*" she challenged me again and again. It was clear that much of the institutionalized racism she lives with every day was pretty much news to me, hard as it is for me to admit that.

Abashed, I am getting a late education as we speak.

Another extended conversation I've been having is about intimacy and sex, and how the society has defined what is acceptable and what is not. This friend is an adventurous fellow in his prime who wants to explore the ways love and longing get tangled up for him when the imposed social norms of our society go against his best instincts.

As you might imagine, this dialogue is quite a bit easier, not to mention more fun than the conversations on racism, but equally essential as we ask ourselves some hard questions about what is natural and healthy human behavior, and what is not.

In both conversations it feels as if we are committing a kind of heresy, outing subjects at a level of personal transparency long considered *verboten*. We are letting in light where shadows have covered things up, braving the dark closets of the mind and heart by asking hard questions about our own old, worn-out assumptions.

It's a breath of fresh air, for sure!

I feel as if we're probing for the Shadow *behind* the shadows for that deep source of angst that lies beneath the veneer of our self-images and approved desires.

So, taking a closer look at both male dominance and institutional racism, which are undoubtedly connected, the Shadow seems to really be about insecurity and the deep fear of losing control. Men, mostly, have found their personal power by wresting ownership of women, of slaves, of property—becoming the "Lords of the Land."

From that has followed social and economic hierarchies that define human beings as private property, and thus for sale at a profit, and the men have the power to write that into the Law. This inevitably allows for legalized disrespect—also called 'slavery'—and its attendant forms of torture, in which whole segments of the population get defined as secondary or sub-human and are treated accordingly.

Thus it happens that greed and control have been protected by the rules of the privileged class, which in this country now means mostly white people. These rules are in virtually nobody's true interest, but yet are accepted as the Law of the Land. The reality is that *everyone* suffers, the primary victims along with the rest of us who bear witness to their victimization.

Even the ruling class suffers, even though they may not cop to it.

The resulting horror is the sense of personal failure and self-hate so many in our society walk around with. Few of us are immune to it, whatever our class, gender, body type, or skin color.

Ugh.

Taking a look at the subject of sex and intimacy, the Shadow behind the shadows seems to be a deep fear of nature's wildness: the body itself, desire, sexual surrender, death, even though we all feel a powerful longing for physical connection with the earth and one another. Again, the problem seems to be about power and control, trying to tame the natural world through denial or defining it as a commodity to be mined for profit—raped, in other words—and calling the natural impulses of our bodies shameful sins we should be punished for.

Ironic.

The result is a disconnection from Nature, a fear of love, sexuality and death, and the sense of frustrated impotence that follows. We experience it as 'self-hate.'

I know another story that is about both race and love at the same time. It happened many years ago that a friend's (white) mother had a secret affair with an African-American man who was a friend of the family, and she became pregnant as a result. This was before either abortion or mixed marriages were legal. She was terrified of what might be revealed at the birth of this child, and was an emotional wreck during her whole pregnancy. Nobody had any idea what the problem was, my friend told me.

I remember that once the baby was born—a lovely honey-colored little girl with big black eyes—she was so entrancing she won the hearts of everyone who laid eyes on her. As if she knew her life depended on it, she played to her public from the very beginning, an adorable as well as totally adored little charmer.

I will never know what my friend's father thought when he saw this newborn baby emerge from his wife's body, but he took her as his own without missing a beat. The child's probable actual father remained a friend of the family and often came to visit with gifts for all the kids, never forgetting the birthday of the child he must have known was his.

I've often wondered if there were ever confrontations between the adults. Did they seek counseling, separately or together; did they ever speak about it with their other children? Did the other man's wife suspect? Did the girl herself ever wonder if maybe he might be …? According to my friend, the subject never really came up.

"She was our baby sister," was what she told me. "We all were totally crazy about her."

So there you are—that's the power of new life and love.

New possibilities. New opportunities.

It's good stuff to talk about.

My Family History

I am still steeped in my recollections of the past, my own and the world's, and trying to hold fear at bay as fire season in the West comes closer, with wildfires already burning in the Southwest—and it is only May! My friends in Santa Fe have been manning the front lines, trying to protect their world and one another as the winds change and the fires leap. The only way I know to help them is to write about fear itself, which is up and real for me—and probably most of us—right now. How do we face a world so burning with uncertainties?

How do I?

It brings me right back to childhood, when I was always scared the grownups would finally blaze over the edge and burn themselves up, taking all us kids with them. These people were out of control with fear, my relatives who had barely made it out of the Russian *shtetels* alive, hidden beneath their mother's skirts on ships loaded with refugees to the new country of America. It was clear we kids—my three boy cousins, my sister, and me—were not safe with the grown-ups because they were truly crazy. Their desperation was well-justified, and their stories horrific, so we kids had to watch out and know when to run!

Clara, our Alpha female, went to funerals of strangers to find release, using the old-country mode of hysterical shrieking and tearing her hair when she needed to vent. I wondered what those other families must have felt when they saw her coming, for surely she had a reputation in our part of town. At my father's funeral she literally climbed in on top of him in the open casket, hollering for him to wake up and drive her home! This, after first going into the wrong viewing room and jumping onto another family's beloved corpse! We heard her through the walls, and it took four of us to get her out of there and into the right room, apologizing like mad to all the horrified folks on our way out.

Vey iss mir! as we say in Yiddish.

Her hoarse battle shouts of that fateful day were the same ones she had used for chasing us kids down the block, one slipper in hand to smack us with when she caught us. "Get over here so I can kill you!" she would holler as we raced around the corner and scrambled under the hedges to hide.

In fact, she never killed anyone (although she did once push a pregnant daughter-in-law down a flight of stairs because she was jealous) but every last one of us was dependent on her for our survival. In truth, she earned her madness honestly as the eldest of five sisters escaping from certain death in Russia, huddled in the folds of their mother's long skirt. Twice, as one sister had glaucoma and they were all sent back to Russia from Ellis Island the first time!

In our family we had no Alpha males; they were either "overseas" in the war or already dead. The older ones still home were silent men who spoke rarely, and I never saw them cry except for when two soldiers came to the door with a Purple Heart in a box, to tell us that my favorite uncle Leon, my mother's brother, was dead.

We kids never forgot we were refugees who talked funny, kept hard secrets and sobbed helplessly in the bathroom when the war news was on the radio. Our 'boys' were in Europe fighting Hitler—many never coming back—and the women were going mad or worse back home. The kids either acted out like crazy, or faded into the wallpaper and watched.

I was the one who faded into the wallpaper.

I mostly kept secret my longing to dance because someone had to be there for the others, so I sat by the sidelines and watched the others play in the street, knowing better than to run around like a kid.

"See how nice she sits, doesn't bother anybody," Clara would say, praising my hard-won paralysis. "Do like she does and don't bother me!"

Our family may have been extreme, but we weren't alone with this and we came by it honestly, as we'd already lost my favorite uncle Leon to the war, and my grandmother Sarah was already confined to a wooden wheelchair in a "Home for Jewish Incurables," paralyzed from the neck down with Multiple Sclerosis. I spent every Sunday of my life there, and "The Home," as we called it, still haunts my dreams.

Her own mother, Bubbe, was killed by a truck while shopping on Delancey Street, the Shabbos chicken still hanging in a bag from her wrist, and Clara's sister Francis, who was the reason they had been turned back at Ellis Island the first time they tried to come in, later poisoned her baby by boiling his teddy-bear in Boric Acid to "sterilize it." My own Mama cried insatiably for her brother, our family light, who died of a septic wound just as the war ended. I still have the post-card he wrote, telling the family he'd be home "any day now."

My father, in his frustration at losing his wife to grief, started coming to me. I had to run fast because his grabbings frightened me, and always made my mother's face get tight and look away. "Leave her …" the women muttered in Yiddish while I struggled to get out of his grasp.

Years later at my wedding, he would slap me across the face in my pretty white dress and lace mantilla, to everyone's shock, and I spent my wedding night sobbing in Herb's arms. "If you've changed your mind, we can annul," I recall choking out to him in despair, "you don't have to marry into my crazy family!" He just held me close as we wept together, our vows safely sealed for the rest of our lives together.

One last story about my father, and then I'll stop: This one took place around the birth of our first child, which my father, in New York, was determined to be at in California, "to make sure someone calls a specialist if anything goes wrong." Convinced it was his right to be in the delivery room with us, he repeated these demands regularly, pestering our doctor as well as the head of the hospital throughout most of my pregnancy. How my stress from that affected our baby in the womb, I still cannot bear to think about, despite Herb's and the doctor's and the Head of the hospital's reassurance that my father would never be allowed into the hospital, much less the delivery room, period!

But they didn't know my father as well as I did, for he had a heart attack in New York exactly when I went into labor in Berkeley, successfully grabbing everyone's attention while I was giving birth to our beautiful boy on the other coast.

I am telling these stories with a purpose. The fact is that I survived all this madness, and may even be the stronger for it, even though I would never recommend it to anyone as a technique. But I learned how to trust my own best instincts until I was free to let go of all that fear and follow my deeper imagination. I learned how to slip around wrong rules and make up my own, and to imagine myself dancing freely on a stage, my dress flaring about my legs as I ran like the wind. Dreaming up fanciful ways of living, I imagined alternatives to what everyone else was doing, even though I nearly flunked out of Elementary School in the process! It was those Multiple Choice tests, of course, as I was convinced all the answers were partly right.

I was a pretty lonely kid and I read insatiably, including Darwin, whose inspiration for the diversity of species caught my imagination early on, and I longed for years to go to the Galápagos Islands where he had seen how species evolved depending upon where they lived and what they had to eat. On the bare lava of volcanic islands, living is not easy, and a plant or a creature had to be very inventive to grab a toe-hold. For years I longed to see it for myself, and finally did in my 30s, tagging onto a group of geologists as a non-scientist on a scientific expedition.

I wanted to observe evolution in action and see all the ways plants and creatures have survived the disasters of the past, changing themselves to match challenging new conditions, creatively finding ingenious ways to live. Like me. On this tiny archipelago off the coast of South America, enough species of plants, birds, lizards and insects did this successfully enough to adapt and creatively try out life in a new place, evolving a unique ecosystem on barren shores.

The result, all these eons later, is what is recognized as a laboratory of evolution: If there's nothing to eat on all this black lava, why don't we try jumping back into the sea to eat algae on offshore rocks? (marine iguanas...) If the ocean is full of fish and we can dive for them, who needs big wings to fly? (flightless cormorants...)

That's what I'm keeping my eye on now: How to adapt to scary changes in the world. How can we take them on cunningly, rather than trying to fight them? Like iguanas and cormorants, how can we each be creative, swerving around obstacles in an unknown sea and finding other daring folks to swim with us? If creative solutions to brand new problems worked to keep lizards and cormorants alive on barren lava, why don't we try a human version for ourselves?

That's how change has always happened, both by chance and by design. Personally, I see it happening all around me when I look for it. I tend to keep an eye out for where the fun and chaos are, because that's where I find brand new solutions pouring out of the ground like geysers.

Have you noticed how skateboards have morphed from a quick ride to school to an art form by kids in just a few short years? Their bodies and minds have evolved before our eyes from straightaway skateboard-ing to swerving and jumping over obstacles, surfing concrete waves to the top and leaping into thin air, flying!

They seem to love learning new ways to balance, defying what we assume to be 'gravity.' Personally, I wonder if they are helping to expand our ordinary definition of Nature itself!

I am wondering if that's what it's all about now, taking the risk to extend our imaginations and recognize that our Universe is a lot larger and more complex than we've been assuming all this time. The young ones are doing it—it's already here—but so are the detractors, who often are nobody but ourselves, because we're scared to take those leaps of faith.

But it's time … it's time to take our chances!

Please—it is time! And there is no time to waste.

Human Nature

Twelve years ago, coming home from the movies one night I made one of the biggest mistakes of my life—I ran over a woman riding a motor scooter. In the dark street, I simply didn't see her.

I had caught her on the shoulder and she was pinned beneath my car, helpless. By the time the ambulance arrived, she had passed out and I thought she was dead.

After she'd been extricated by the ambulance crew and taken away, the police held me hostage until they heard from the hospital that she had survived. I trembled uncontrollably for several hours, 'knowing' now what it was like to have taken someone's life, and my own life was changed forever by that knowing.

Thank goodness she lived, but for the year it took for lawyers and insurance agents to negotiate the case, I was allowed no information: neither to know her name nor what hospital she was in nor the status of her injuries. I could not even send her a Get Well card because legally we were now enemies, and the issue now was about how much money she could get from me! I argued for compassion and common sense, but nobody would budge on the 'rules' until the 'case was settled.'

It was hell.

I had made a serious error and now was in helpless terror with no way of resolving my error. Interesting that terror and error are almost the same word, don't you think?

If an error is not used for learning, I found out, it becomes impotent terror.

Unable to reach out to her was an insult to both of us, but that was the law, a law that assumes we cannot trust one another and therefore must be protected from each other.

I still want to scream at the inhumanity of it all. We two women had an accident and badly needed to help each other through a hard time, but the system would not allow it.

All these years later, as our society goes seriously off the rails, I'm asking how we ever collectively got to such a pass. Is it just human nature to behave with small-minded fear of one another, or have we been provoked to respond that way, and if so, when in our history did that attitude get set?

I've been wondering, lately, about our culture's competitive, God-fearing mindset and where it came from. Why have we allowed ourselves to be controlled into believing we were all out to get one another? So I keep looking for the ancient sources of early belief systems—like the Abrahamic tradition, for example, before it became three distinct 'religions'—and asking what came *before* in the deserts of Judaea?

There I find the Gnostics, a small early-Christian sect that worshiped the Mysteries through the sacred earth herself—Gaia-Sophia. When they had to flee for their lives, routed by other more warlike sects, they apparently hid their scriptures for safe-keeping in a cave in the Nag Hammadi hills. There the texts lay unknown for over 2000 years until quite recently, when they were discovered in crumbling jars by two shepherds wandering the hillside with their sheep.

Alas, many pages were used as kindling before the finds were recognized as important—or worth money!

After almost fifty years of frantic fights between Biblical scholars in the 'civilized' world about who owned these codices and who had a right to see them, they were finally apportioned out and carefully reproduced and translated, fragment by fragment, making their way gradually into texts the rest of us could read and ponder.

The essence of Gnostic teaching is that the Mystery is available to all human beings through direct intuition, as we all have the Divine endowment of knowing, ourselves, 'what the Gods know.' The earth itself and everything upon it is sacred, and Divine intelligence is inherent in all beings. It says we must have full confidence in this inborn inheritance and therefore must use ourselves well for the good of all.

What a breath of fresh air!

This is a far cry from teachings that begin with a wrathful, jealous God who has the power to judge and punish, demand obedience with violence and define sin as just about everything that comes naturally. As sinners, we then require redemption and salvation from Above, especially from the ultimate sin—being born of a woman!

Eve's sin—but … how else …?

Of course institutions based upon such a skewed view of the human soul will then be adversarial. How could they be otherwise? Why would we trust anyone as sinful as ourselves?

It's time to take stock, now. We can see where that has led, century by century, and it is more than time to change—before the Earth Herself forces the issue for us!

So, back to my story.

After a year of waiting for my 'case' to be settled, I was permitted to write a letter to her through her lawyer, introducing myself as the person who ran over her and expressing my wish to make peaceful contact. Her positive response, through him, came immediately.

What an extraordinary afternoon we spent together! She arrived with flowers in her arms, and we sat in my garden exchanging stories and holding hands: we talked about what happened that night to each of us; her injuries and hospital stays; what this hard year had been like for both of us, and the fact that even on that fateful night, she did not blame me.

Bless her.

We got giddy, and made crazy jokes with lines like, "We *can't* keep bumping into each other like this ..." or "I like you a lot—I'm SO glad I didn't kill you!"

We laughed and we cried, and hugged each other, unable to let go. And agreed that the system that had kept us apart for a whole year *had* to be changed.

As far as I know, it has not.

I learned a lot in that year, and so much is relevant these days as we experience the inevitable train wreck of this presidency. I wonder about our passive consent, over the years, to legal and religious systems that tell us that we are not to trust one another; that our natural instincts are dangerous; that the idea of intuitive intelligence based upon the laws of nature is *woo-woo*.

If so, it's time to stop assuming that we must consent to ideas we do not believe in, and to actively ask some pretty obvious questions:

Do we humans make mistakes?

Of course we do.

Can we learn from our mistakes?

We can and had better do so.

Are we capable of knowing and loving ourselves and each other so well that we all benefit?

You'd better believe it!

Why have we forgotten the obvious truth of this for such a long time?

Good question.

Freeflow Stories

in memoriam, Alick Bartholomew

Finally, real rain! It pelts against the roof and gushes down the drainpipes, turning our dry turf to mud and flowing like a river down the street. Children, all booted up, splash in the puddles.

My mood has shifted from grief to relief. Our drought is over—for now, at least.

I can feel myself relax in stages, starting with my tears when the first rains came; and then the unclogging of the kitchen sink; and then the greening of our gardens that seemed to happen overnight. The more I relax, it seems, the more the synchronicities happen, and most of them these days have to do with water!

Apparently something is pointing me in Water's direction right now, a fascination I have been dipping into (pardon the pun) periodically all my life. It's time again.

I dream of fountains that won't turn off; I discover a faucet leaking downstairs; and I learn of the death of a Scottish researcher whose inspiring writings on water I have followed for several years—Alick Bartholomew.

That story actually began several years ago, one day when I was walking home from the bookstore after trying unsuccessfully to find a copy of his new book on water. Meeting a neighbor, we stopped to chat and I mentioned the book I was out looking for, my interest in the subject of water and how important this author's work was to me, and that he lived in a small village in England. She laughed.

"You may not believe it, but he's my father," she said. Of course she was joking—we were backyard neighbors in California and she spoke with an American accent, and we mostly chatted about the cats and the children over the back fence—but my hero was indeed her father!

We both had a good laugh, she offered to write him in England and ask for a copy of his new book for her neighbor, and soon the coveted book arrived with a cordial note from the author!

We had a brief correspondence, and I am sad to know he is no longer amongst us.

Water and synchronicities: both flow from an unknown, immaterial source, both shift and change like will o' wisps and neither are under our control. They both seem to slip from the invisible to the visible and back again, connecting up our tangible world where we carry on our daily lives, with the unseen realms of dreams and visions.

Now you see it, now you don't.

This elusive slipstream of 'there but not quite there' is where my imagination loves to reside, and I spend many of my working hours exploring ways into that subtle territory. That is where definitions are fluid, and I have to sense my way intuitively, rather than *think* my way into meaning.

Singing and dancing are my favorite ways of inhabiting that territory, especially improvised ensemble singing with three or four people, all making it up and riding the remarkable wave of music that emerges from the group, absolutely different each time, always as rich and complex as structured compositions. Our voices seem to emerge effortlessly and meld, until we feel we are the music itself, being sung.

45

It spills forth from us like free-flowing water.

I've been doing this with people for years and the song is always magical, always new and it bonds the singers to one another for good, it seems. We spill between the seen and the unseen, feeling for where the sounds pass from what is invisible and inchoate to where they become art, and the beauty finds and uses us. The experience is ecstatic.

I am reminded of a letter Albert Einstein supposedly wrote to his daughter late in his life, about love:

> *There is an extremely powerful force that so far, science has not found a formal explanation to. It is a force that includes and governs all others, and is even behind any phenomenon operating in the universe and has not yet been identified by us. This universal force is LOVE.*
>
> *Each individual carries within them a small but powerful generator of love whose energy is waiting to be released.*
>
> *When we learn to give and receive this universal energy, dear Lieserl, we will have affirmed that love conquers all, is able to transcend everything and anything, because love is the quintessence of life.*

Sigh...yes...

He knew more than mathematics, Einstein did!

Change!

in memory of Alan Balsam M.D.

By the cricks in my knees, the forgetfulness of my brain and the face that looks back at me in the mirror, it is clear that I am aging. Kneeling in the garden is a thing of the past and so is chocolate before bedtime.

I fear that coming to terms with inevitable change is what's up now, and *fear* is the operative word here. Everything is up for grabs as the world spirals out of control, scaring us witless.

I remember the night I went into labor with our first child, that moment when I realized this wasn't just one night's big adventure. Once this baby was born everything, but *everything* would change! Laboring, on that stormy night in winter, was a precipitous voyage on an unknown sea with high winds and wild waves that went on and on before finally landing me exhausted, but safe upon a new shore.

I remember my good friend and doctor, Alan Balsam, holding up our son as he emerged from my body and calling out,

"What kind of baby do you have?" and me gasping back, "A boy baby!" And then he laid that squalling creature on my stomach, still attached by a spiraling umbilical cord, and I burst into tears as my life irrevocably changed forever.

We're all in a birthing process now, after a centuries long and painful labor that have seen war and revolution, bloody Crusades and runaway injustice going back to the dawn of written history. Like it or not we're all having contractions, trying to catch our breaths and go with the waves of pain as this new era struggles to be born.

These days, as our collective 'labor' heats up, I've been asking myself questions about things I passively have given my consent to every day—as most of us do, really. Like the assumptions of privilege taken by people with light skin; like an economy based on personal profit; like the Earth for sale, parcel by parcel, to the highest bidder; like patriarchal religions that define us as sinful.

I saw a film last night, "Traces From The Trade, a Story from the Deep North," about the slave trade in Rhode Island. It was made by a young descendant of a family that made its wealth as slave traders generations ago. The family mansion still stands tall, white pillars and all, in the center of their quaint New England town.

The filmmaker, Katrina Brown, says, "Of course we all knew about the past, but until now none of us ever bothered to *really know.*" So she courageously decided to find out, and along with eight of her relatives, made a voyage that traced the family's slave-trade route from Rhode Island to Ghana to Cuba.

They indeed found traces, many still right there on the ground: small holding cells in a dungeon where 1000 people at a time were shackled until they could be baptized with Christian names for the auction block. (The church where the baptisms took place was built right on top of the dungeons!)

They found the plantation owned by their ancestors, where sugarcane, to make the rum traded to transport those people across the ocean from Africa, was grown—by slaves! They found the site of the marketplace where men, women and children, oiled to shine for potential buyers, were displayed, sold and taken away.

How amazingly clever we humans can be!

We're built, it seems, for ingenuity on the grand scale—*on the one hand. On the other hand,* however, we have the potential to deviate, to use our genius for evil. It is as if something goes awry, a crack in the imagination where evil can seep in, gain a foothold and twist reason into monstrous cruelty, turning the human heart frigid.

Who—*us?*

The resulting mayhem is coming to a head now, thick and fast. How do we parry with this shocking inhumanity as we are forced to confront the evil entering the world through our own species? Can we meet it straight on and intercept the pattern?

I will not believe evil is inherent to our human souls! But I *do* believe that we may be unsuspecting hosts of the 'virus of evil,' however we catch it.

Alan Balsam and I were both in our 20s when we met at a party in the 1960s. That evening we chatted mostly about body-mind medicine, a subject that at the time hardly existed on anybody's radar. We agreed that healing was about addressing the whole person—body, mind, heart and spirit. I remember that he poured me a glass of wine from a jug over his shoulder—I found that enchanting—I told him I was newly pregnant, introduced him to my husband and we asked if he would be our family physician.

From then on, along with my regular appointments, he and I met in his office every few weeks to do our own explorations. We wondered how emotions affected the healthy functioning of the body, how the body revealed what the heart was feeling. He asked about my dreams that, in my pregnant state, ran the gamut from nightmares to ecstatic visions.

He taught me about the autonomic nervous system and how the body responds to stress. It was he who taught me that the stresses in our bodies could be linked to the common wisdoms we took for granted in our society—that men were stronger than women; that processed food tasted better than fresh; that money was the only way to a good life. We asked questions about drugs and health and dreams. He encouraged us both to ask questions, to always ask questions.

I now do that questioning on my own, as Alan died long before his time. I miss him still, and would give a lot for us to still be talking about how fearfulness manifests through our collective autonomic nervous system, making us weak and reactive when strong, imaginative collaborations should be the order of the day.

Alan and I would have aged together, still challenging the system and agreeing that healthy bodies required the foundation of a healthy society based on justice and emotional wellbeing, in order to function well.

That they go together is so obvious, I wonder how we keep missing it: Love and tenderness, relationship and kindness, compassion and comfort and care—I believe that's how we confront the forces of evil in ourselves as well as in the world.

It sounds too simple, but it isn't...

Alan, I still miss you fiercely!

Harmony and Hope

for Rebecca

Today I weeded the strawberry patch at my brother's farm, Red Clover, and it felt like I was weeding myself as well. Pull a weed, remember a hurt from childhood. As I toss it on the mulch pile, memories crowd my throat and the tears fall.

It is early Spring here in Vermont, the world has turned a tender green, the waterfalls are thundering, and the weeds are trying to take over the gardens. I'm down on my knees in Red Clover's perennial flowerbeds and scrabbling at stubborn roots, my own included.

I love weeding. It's like a meditation as I feel for the plant's grip in the soil and pull with just the right pressure, however deep it goes. I get calm, focused—needing to, these days, as the climate swings wildly from too cold to too hot and society swings wildly from sane to insane.

We're way out of whack. Five young people I know committed suicide recently. But still, the air here is fragrant with lilac and lily of the valley, and last night's thunder-and-lightning storm was a thrilling show!

Where is the balance point?

Last week I was in Boston for my daughter's production "Harmony and Hope," a concert/ritual for healing the deep wounds of gun

51

violence. It was held at a historic church in Roxbury, designed to ease pain in the community and to give hope for a non-violent future.

Partly first-person testimony and partly performance, it began with one mother's story about losing her son to gang warfare. In the shocked silence, the string quartet played Debussy, and we sat close together, tears falling. Then the Gospel singers, hidden in the congregation, stood, one by one singing "Amazing Grace," rousing us to healing tears, as the next speaker spoke of the violent deaths of his best friends. "There were five of us; we grew up together. Now there are only two of us."

We listened to stories of unthinkable loss, and then sat in grieving silence as music again entered the sanctuary, helping us all to weep; then again, more stories, followed by the cleansing ritual of music. And again.

By the time the string quartet and Gospel singers came together for the closing song of hope, "Oh Happy Day" the spirit in the room—the holy sanctuary—was high enough to raise the roof, everyone rocking and clapping and singing together.

The concert/ritual was visionary and perfect, and was created by this child of my heart.

How many ways are there to kneel and kiss the ground? Rumi asks. How many ways to use the gifts of this world, even when they do not look like gifts?

I think about this while pulling dandelions by their strong taproots. On the one hand, I am clearing space for Deb's garden, but on the other, dandelions are actually potent medicinal plants, and healthy food—not to mention beautiful meadow flowers in the rolling green grass of springtime Vermont. I could just as easily be harvesting them for supper, or putting them in a vase.

Why call them *weeds*? Who says they are expendable? Who says guns in the hands of teenagers—especially if they are mostly murdering their own kind—is okay? Why should this even be a discussion?

As it happens, I went canoeing this week in the Adirondack Mountains with my old friend Wendy—and since the summer season had not yet officially started, we had a whole lake to ourselves. Oh, blessed mountain silence by a calm lake and sky, as far as the eye could see.

We were all but alone there, as the summer season had not yet officially started; and unpacking our first picnic lunch, we realized neither of us had thought to bring utensils. No way to cut bread, spread peanut butter, scoop jam!

But we had celery stalks, we realized, so these became our spoons and dippers and spreaders! Of course. When the celery stalks became sticky with peanut butter, hummus and grape jam at the end of our lunch, we ate them up and had a whole new culinary experience! Raw green veggie, peanuts, beans, olive oil, lemon, garlic and grapes in a single bite was a new taste sensation—and whyever not? I would never have thought to put them together, but they were delicious!

The origin of *tapas!*

Artists have always known how to use whatever was available to create their works of art, from patchwork quilts designed from worn out pants to symphonies based on folksongs. All it takes is a creative imagination and a willingness to do the unexpected, whatever that might look like. In Yiddish, that creative imagination is called *chutzpah!*

Every one of us is an artist, Alonzo King says, and it may be more important than ever to get creative, as the challenges are coming at us like fastballs across the tennis net. With the will to do so, we can use that same energy and bat the balls back across the net with all the ingenuity we can muster. The trick is to create new beauty with fun and *chutzpah;* to turn guns into plowshares!

Who knows, maybe that's what this time in the world is really all about? What if we stepped back and took a look at the larger context, the longer arc of change we find ourselves in the midst of? What if we trusted that there might well be a greater meaning to this time in the world, and that what is happening is more of an opportunity than a mistake?

Who knows, maybe Trump, more of a parody than anything believable, is a great actor and part of a much larger production designed to help us wake up?

Why not? This is my life—and yours—and I have no wish to waste it. Mr. Plump or not, our chance is Now and, as Rumi says, there are hundreds of ways to kneel and kiss the ground.

I am falling on my knees ... and hear the angel voices ....

Lonely in America

for Giulio Perrone

It is almost two years since Herb's death, and I miss him terribly—the shared minutia of our daily lives, the small intimacies of touch and affection. I miss his daily phone call from work and the funny *haikus* he would leave for me on the kitchen table.

I miss adoring and being adored.

This week an old colleague of Herb's came to town, someone we've known—me at a distance—for years. Like Herb, she is a poet as well as scientist, and she invited me to catch up over drinks at her hotel. I was pleased she had reached out and looked forward to talking with her outside the 'science' she shared with my husband.

But it was not what I expected. I found myself playing 'audience' to her 'recitative' rather than participating in a two-way conversation. I'd been looking forward to real exchange between women and not one of those mutual monologues that so often pass for conversation in our society.

So I did what I do—I asked leading questions and tried to look interested. Once, when I started to express my own thoughts she talked over me to signal the waiter for another drink. The timing was too perfect, and I was cut to the quick.

"I'll wait," I said quietly, but she never cued me back in. Clearly, I'd been invited to be a listener.

Maybe she was lonely and just needed someone to talk to. Perhaps she wanted a woman's ear to pour out some hard relationship stuff to—which she did. Whatever it was, I got bored and eventually I smiled goodnight and went home.

Oh, if I could have told the whole story to Herb!

The real exchange we all long for, the meeting of minds and hearts seems to be a rare bird in our society, and most of us walk around lonely much of the time, longing for authentic connection.

It has happened lately that several friends—men and women of all the stripes—have confessed to me their love problems: either they long to find their perfect partner, or they want to leave their imperfect partner.

I'm reminded of that poignant scene in "Fiddler in the Roof" in which one of Tevye's daughters sings,

> *Matchmaker, matchmaker,*
> *Make me a match…*

As I come from those same Russian-Jews in the 'old country,' I know that the resulting matches were far from ideal, to say the least. My ancestors were not happy people.

So how do we find one another to love?

I wish everyone could have it happen by a crazy chance, as it did with Herb and me, two Jews meeting at a Midnight Mass in an Anglican Church on Christmas Eve in New York City, tickled to catch one another's eye in a crowd of well-dressed Episcopalians. It was like Oberon and Puck playing tricks on us at night in the forest, bringing us together when we least expected it. What if we all had playful fairies working on our behalf to find us our own true loves?

The magic of connection actually happened in real time yesterday at a free production of Midsummer Night's Dream by The Inferno Theater, outdoors in a local park. I'd already seen it the week before, but came again because I was so moved the first time! The sets were a couple of sheets strung across bamboo poles, the young actors were a diverse group of gifted actor/acrobats and the action was swift, hilarious and all over the place!

It was true *Commedia dell'Arte*.

Shakespeare would have loved it! In my favorite scene, the players-within-the-play came out barking from behind dog masks, their fake doggy ears swinging. This caused a real doggy in the audience to bark back, so the actors played along and returned his barks. Soon every dog in the park was barking and then the audience joined in, barking crazily in an impromptu scene Shakespeare never anticipated!

Laughing, we shared exclamations with folks on the next blanket, offering cookies and commentary.

Barking, we bonded. It was that easy. Woof!

After the show, I looked for the Director to compliment him on the staging and ask how he worked. The show was so tight, so funny, such an enchantment!

"Let's have tea," was Giulio's response.

We did. At my house later in the week he told me it was all about relationship between the cast and the audience. Scenes were choreographed to create bonds between the actors and between the actors and the audience.

"Each audience is different," he explained. "The actors can read each audience from the beginning by how they respond, and then they play to them. You want to make the experience real in the moment—felt, physical, emotional."

He went on, "The actors have to have the technique to start with, of course, and then the work is to open their hearts and encourage their bodies to move together. Then you wait for the magic to happen."

We were quiet together for awhile, pondering. Then he said,

"It's a good way to do the work of the world, don't you think? And these kids are so wonderful at it!"

"Yes. I get the feeling they understand just how important their work is—bigger than just being on the stage."

"The arts are the key to the Big Work we have to do," he said musingly.

"Yes," I agreed. "Thank you for what you do, helping us all find the unexpected connections and to meet one another in a new place." He made a small bow and returned the compliment.

"I am so glad to know you," I added, touching his arm and taking another sip of tea. We smiled conspiratorially at one another.

"Two peas in a pod," he said.

Who knows, maybe the two of us will dream up a collaboration one of these days?

Woof! Woof!

Now What Should
We Talk About?

for Pema Chödrön

Less than fifty years ago, when I was camping on the shore of Fernandina Island in the Galápagos, I awoke at dawn each day to a sky mobbed with birds: blue-footed and masked boobies, pelicans, frigate birds. On the rocks, tropical penguins jostled with flightless cormorants for diving space, everyone gobbling up breakfast from the fish-filled sea.

It suspect it was what the whole world once looked like.

Today, walking down by the Marina, I could count on one hand the number of birds out there. I've tried to pretend that maybe they were migrating, maybe they were resting … but I know better. I've been taking morning walks here for years, and the sky has never been this empty.

I am in mourning, as if for family.

I've always wondered how long it would take us to wake up to the reality of an 'ending time'—the Great Turning, as Joanna Macy calls it—being like frogs in the boiling pot, not catching on until it was *almost* too late.

I'm rather slow at catching on, myself … like this morning when I couldn't remember where I put my glasses …

And where'd the notebook I wanted to write in about the forget-fulness of aging go? Why can't I find the novel I want to spend the morning reading—rereading, actually? I *need* to melt into the calming world of Elizabeth Goudge on this chilly Sunday morning, curled up in bed as the world goes crazy, and I cannot put my hand on the darned book!

It's laughable, really, but I take it hard.

I am reminded of a conversation I had with Pema Chödrön many years ago, long before she was Pema. We'd known one another as teenagers on the other side of the country, completely lost contact and then surprised each other in Berkeley at the neighborhood play-ground, each with kids in tow.

It just so happened that we both lived near the Tot Lot, that our children were close in age, and that we were both students of Bud-dhism—she in the Tibetan tradition, me in Zen—so we had lots to talk about. In our twenties and pretty adorable—*she* certainly was, at least—we exchanged news of men and marriage, motherhood, and all the juicy gossip that was going around in the Buddhist community.

This was the early 60s when everyone was experimenting with everything, especially in Berkeley, and we compared notes about it all, including our families' mystification of this meditation 'thing' we were both into. She told me about a relative who objected to her short-cropped hair and insulted her by calling her 'ugly.'

"What'd you say back to *her?*" I asked.

"I went over to the mirror, took a good look at myself and said, 'By golly, you're right! Now what should we talk about?'"

We broke up laughing and ran to rescue a child hanging by her ankles from the swing.

I keep remembering that wonderful line now, whenever we—the Democrats especially—act shocked by the President's latest inanities, even though it is clear he is what he is—an out-of-control two-year old with power. Anyone who has ever parented a two-year old knows that you keep your cool when he screams and demands to play with the hammer, hand him his Teddy to distract him and calmly go back to baking the cookies. That's how we set limits for him—by being the adults in the room and letting him learn how far he can go without hurting himself—not to mention all the rest of us.

That's our job. And his job is to make us do *our* job. Obama tried hard to get us to do our job, but we mostly relaxed on his watch. Now we've been forced to take on the work because if we don't, it's curtains!

So now what should we talk about?

Maya Angelou says, "We need to remember that we are created creative, and can invent new scenarios as frequently as they are needed."

I think it's time that we all invent those new scenarios together, getting very creative, very specific, and very visionary. I believe it has to start with each one of us delving deep into our own wounds and being willing to do the work of healing ourselves—for starters.

Pema and I, in those early years, were both seekers. We knew that our practices had to start with our own masked confusions: our fears, our hurt places, our stories. We questioned our assumptions of white privilege; we looked for the gems hiding in our deep shadows; we tried to make our unconsciousness conscious.

Meditating helped calm us, we agreed, but it was hard because it showed us who we really were, and that did not always feel good. But we knew that however messy the process was, we had no choice because the alternative was way too bleak.

"I'll just make the same mistakes over and over again," she confessed one day.

Me too.

And then she went on to help half the world do the deep work that she personally took on. I bow to her.

I took the householder path—the 'monk' as wife and mother—carrying water and chopping wood in every ordinary way—and then in some not-so ordinary ways.

We've been preparing for this time in the world for ages whether we've known it or not, getting ready for the almost-boiling point when we'd have to either hop out of the pot or get cooked. We'd be naïve to pretend that the pot has just started cooking with this election. It's been heating up for a long, long time—longer than we've been around. Since the Industrial Revolution? Since colonization? Since Abraham walked the earth?

Maybe we're slow learners, but however we want to think about it, the time has more than come for us to change course.

Hopping out of the pot may be just a matter of getting to know ourselves so deeply and honestly that we have the courage to open up and love, no matter what. It may be just that simple and that hard.

Loving, we mysteriously spread a high vibration wherever we go. Without even trying, we become contagious with kindness, spreading it around like fairy dust and magically attracting to us everything we need. I have no idea exactly how it works, but I do know it works, and that it is what ultimately changes the world.

Yes, we're going through the eye of the needle now, but how else do we make the big changes that have to be made? Meditation is just one way, but there are many. My personal preference is dancing and singing and becoming aware of how I really *feel*—body, mind and spirit, even though it is not always pretty.

Easy or hard, when the pot heats up our only choice is to make a move. And then learn all over again how to walk.

Now what should we talk about?

Well, last evening at sunset I went back down to the Bay. The birds were there! Gulls, cormorants, ducks. A few pelicans.

Not in droves, no, but the birds were there.

Fairy Tale

At the bus stop yesterday an angry young woman paced back and forth, ranting along with a foul-mouthed rap song on her gizmo, causing all the rest of us to be watchful and silent. I recognized the quality of her anger, and could only imagine the life story that was behind it. In a strange way, I identified with her need to shout out her hurt and be heard. Like her, I am as angry as anyone about things seemingly out of my control. I wanted not only to help her, but to also do some yelling myself, deliberately shaking up whoever else was around.

It reminded me of the 8th fairy in *Sleeping Beauty*, the so-called bad fairy who was so hurt at not being invited to the Princess's christening that she decided to kill the baby and destroy everyone in the castle.

That would show them!

But in the variant of the story most of us know, the good fairy gets her to simmer down and to think her options.

"Be more creative," she is cautioned. "If they're dead, they're just dead. How about, say, a spinning wheel with a drugged spindle? If the Princess pricks her finger on it, then she and everyone else in the castle falls into a deep sleep for 100 years."

"Oh-ho! I'll make sure she pricks her finger!" snorts the furious fairy.

The mature fairy continues, "If she does that, then, let's see—how about a dense briar thicket that grows up around the castle walls? All thorny and dark …"

"Good!" Exclaims the angry fairy, clasping her hands with a bit too much glee, so her fairy sister, in the interest of sanity and eventual peace, suggests a brave and handsome prince who will one day, but far in the future, hack through the briars, climb through a shut window, rescue the Sleeping Princess and wake her with a gentle kiss.

And so it was.

I love both these fairies, especially the quick thinker with a soft touch, an improviser dreaming up scenarios in which everyone has a chance of coming out whole.

I'd like to be her right now, seeing the humor in my situation and taking it on with poise and elan. But I'm not there yet. My body still aches, my heart has not yet made peace with what I witness of destructive madness in the world.

Despite myself, I register the helpless shock of watching madness unfold at the hands of fearful and ignorant (mostly) men, destroying lives wantonly without a qualm. "These are my people!!" I want to shout, clutching the children in my arms and kicking the bullies, who would harm them, hard in their kneecaps! I do not suffer fools gladly, and I am horrified that people I count on for protection let them get away with it!

I am not easy to be around these days.

The good fairy, though, is watching this whole scenario with some amusement, occasionally calling out, "You go girl!" But mostly reminding me that the world is still learning how to grow up and we are in an immature phase of a long process that will not last forever.

"Watch yourself," she counsels me with a smile. "Not everyone can handle you on fire, so notice those who can. They're your tribe. Keep them close and stay true to your own path. Think of this as a turning point on that road you all are treading together, like it or not. It's a test and perhaps it is inevitable if we are all to wake up together. And I mean ALL! Yes, it's getting harder out there and you'll want to travel with the ones you can count on, so now's the time to identify them."

"But it can be so lonely!" I complain.

"Yup," she replies with not a trace of pity. "So when the rage and isolation come up, note what you feel. Study it well, because that is what we all feel when others make us invisible; when we are victims of injustice; when we feel unloved and vulnerable."

I sighed, and the good fairy sighed too, shrugging her iridescent wings and adding, "Get to know those feelings so deeply that when others cry out their despair, you can recognize what they are feeling from your own experience. Like that, you will be able to help."

"But I can be so mean and nasty!"

"Oh, you know you're not basically a mean person, so enjoy it for a while. Get it out of your system. Be ironically amused by just how nasty you can get. That's how you'll know what it feels like inside, and why people do the crazy things they do. Just like you, they're hurting."

"But what if I burn too many bridges in the process?" I whine.

"Well, then don't. Be discriminating where you spread your nasties. Be in your snit while it's sizzling, but take some responsibility for the outcomes. You can do that."

"Some days, maybe," I grumble. The good fairy laughs, rather enjoying my discomfort.

"Listen, honey," she says, "It's hard out there now and it's gonna get harder. You know that. People are hurting now, but just wait until the temperature climbs out of reach and the water is all but gone. You think you've seen craziness so far? You haven't seen nothin' yet! You and all your friends are going to be needed—this is preparation time."

"Who asked for it?" I mumble darkly.

"Probably you and everyone alive on the planet now did. Have you noticed the new ones coming in, how quickly they are growing up, how wise they seem to be? Watch them, and help them. Be patient with yourself, and be there for the young."

"I need a nap!"

"Then take one, and when you wake up, go back to learning from your experience. Use your anger well. Shout out rap songs at bus stops and memorize how it feels to be naughty and shunned by the other passengers. Laugh at yourself when you can, so you remember to do so. Take every moment of this training program seriously, but be careful not to take yourself too seriously."

"Whut?"

"Yup, it's just one damn conundrum after another, isn't it? Think about it—you'll figure it out. Meanwhile, good luck. I'll be here if you need me. Just try not to kill anyone off in the process, okay?"

And in a whiff of fairy smoke, she was gone.

The Fire Next Time

The October fires that we fear each year, fanned by the Santa Ana winds that whip the dry landscape into racing flames, have hit us hard. Whole areas of Sonoma County are devastated and the number of displaced, injured and missing people is growing daily. Some of these folks are people I know and love.

So far our farm, just a few short miles south and west of the burn area is smoky, but not in flames. I get the news second hand, as I am home in Berkeley worrying, getting hints of the fire's progress by how thick the overcast is here, how the air smells.

In days gone by the native peoples, following the natural cycles, did controlled burns on a regular basis to encourage new growth and help the natural ecology refresh itself, skillfully diverting the flames to protect the areas of their encampments. As stewards of their ecosystems they knew how to manage the land so as to maintain its health and productivity, and therefore their own.

We've unfortunately forgotten how, and are now paying for our ignorance.

Many years ago, in the aftermath of a great forest fire in the Los Padres National Forest near Big Sur, the photographer Robert Boni and I decided to do a book on the re-emergence of a burned-out forest—his photographs, my text. We wanted to follow the stages of regeneration by traipsing in the burn area about every two months, over the course of a year—maybe two—with cameras and tripods, slogging through the ash and taking pictures of the process as life began to re-emerge from the cinders, and the wildlife started finding its way back home.

We had the *best* time, getting totally filthy and watching the miracle of green life reassert itself stage by stage in the acres of burned-out forest. By the end of that year we were witness to a young forest eco-system pushing out of the ground with renewed vigor and growth, taking back the land.

It was like magic!

Then, in 1980, after the massive volcanic eruptions of Mount Saint Helens when *hundreds* of square miles of centuries-old forest were laid waste, Herb and I and the kids went there as soon as tourists were allowed back into the area. It was a heart-stopping moonscape as far as the eye could see, dead and silent.

But not altogether, we discovered as we hiked our way through the tuff. A bee buzzed by us, and following her zig-zag flight we discovered a bit if green poking through the ash, a prairie lupin. Tips of pine and tenacious grass were taking hold, bravely re-asserting their green selves onto the devastation. Once our eyes noticed the green we saw it everywhere!

Now, almost fifty years later the rich lava there fertilizes a new generation of forest eco-system, not identical to the old but in many ways richer and fuller than what was there before.

Sometimes it takes hardship to provoke change, like the shock of a healing crisis that jogs the body onto a path of readjustment and healing. It is a trial by fire, a hard kick in the pants that hurts like hell but provides the shock we need to reset our systems towards health. Maybe it is even the perfect metaphor for our social and political times, a kind of high fever that provides the impetus for a necessary change.

A true healing crisis.

I grieve for all the shock and fear and personal loss around me, and I pray for every being who has unwittingly made such a sacrifice. I wish it did not have to be so, but confusion and the unexpected seem to be the name of the game, despite us.

I hope we can use the experience well.

I remember how quickly, after the big Berkeley/Oakland fire in 1989, the insurance companies and realtors got busy telling the burned-out homeowners what to do next, which was to re-build on the grand scale, sell high for a huge profit and, with big bucks in hand, move elsewhere. Suggestions by city planners and progressive architects to re-think the design so as to foster community by using the 'clean slate' as an opportunity for encouraging mutuality and connection, were ignored.

It broke my heart.

Now, all these years later, we have the opportunity again in Sonoma County. It just so happens that a group of us has been meeting for the last two years to start The CommonSpace Community Land Trust, with the idea of challenging the assumptions of private property and the speculative real estate market. Our plan has been to start with the farm and to model shared, affordable housing on land held in the public trust.

We want to try and demonstrate another way of living together— and we're just about ready to launch this month!

Huge swaths of land in the County have been leveled to the ground by the fires, and the status quo has been definitely disrupted. People are grieving their losses and helping one another get back on their feet. And the community, still in shock, has come together in powerful ways to help.

The time is Now, it seems to me, to plan boldly for new ways of living together, rethinking how we humans might reconfigure community from the rubble of the past. This is not the first time we have built new lives on top of the ruins of the old—over the centuries probably more times than we know—and we have a chance to surprise ourselves with our creativity.

Thanks to Darryl, Kate, Cassandra, Jerry, Sara, Dan and Eden, the folks who are creating the CommonSpace CLT with me. We're having the best time!

It's an ancient story that the Phoenix rises from the ashes, alive and new!

May it be so.

How Much Time Do We Have?

Lately, I've been wondering about civilizations long before ours, curious about long-ago lives that could be resting beneath the seas of the world. I am reading about "mythic cycles of creation and destruction by floods stretching back hundreds of thousands of years," and of ruins recently uncovered in Indonesia dating back 28,000 years, making the pyramids in Egypt seem recent in comparison.

People lived there, loved and died on this same earth we now inhabit. Who were they and what did they know? How many unknown eons of life and experience are hidden beneath our earth and oceans?

How old are we as a species, anyway?

I had lunch recently with a young man I last saw in India when he was four years old, my friend Rumi's little boy. He is now a well-known scientist in California, with his own grown children.

As it happens, his daughter Akaina—Rumi's granddaughter—now lives in Berkeley, so I am one of her 'aunties.' She looks a lot like her *great*-grandma, who I met in Calcutta when Rumi and I stayed with her parents for a week, so I personally know four generations of the same family!

Where did the time go?

As if to emphasize the brevity of our lives, I received a phonecall a short while ago from a teenage boyfriend, James, who was dying and wished to say a last farewell. And thank me for our time together.

"I've a farewell gift for you," he told me in a weak voice. "Remember the string quartet I was writing for you when we were together? I've recorded it and am sending it to you before I die."

I was deeply moved, and also could hear, in my mind's ear, the melody of the First Movement, and I sang it for him over the phone. He listened with held breath, I think, and his wife later told me that he cried while I was singing. I have no idea how I recalled it so clearly and immediately, except that it is truly beautiful. It was my last gift to him, in response to his last gift to me, and for the first time, I was able to tell him that I loved him.

It was during the two years in my late teens that we'd been together that I was reading Teilhard de Chardin, a Jesuit priest who was also both a geologist and paleontologist. His ideas were radical—like my own—and made my Harvard boyfriend see red! I suspect it was this basic bone of contention that convinced me not to marry him.

Teilhard wrote, "The most telling and profound way of describing the evolution of the universe would undoubtedly be to trace the evolution of love." He measured evolution, not in terms of our short human lifetimes, but in terms of rocks and bones resting in the earth for untold millennia.

"Deep hope flows over deep time," he wrote, noting a definite upwards movement towards consciousness on the cosmic scale, however the rising and falling of the human story ran from day to day. He claimed that when we lost sight of this longer pattern, the result was anguish and impatience.

Yes!

I've come, since James, to judge my own evolution by how spontaneously I am able to love, especially when I least expect it, when love slips into crevices I had no idea were there. A child seen on a bus; a woman on the checkout line at a grocery store.

I experience it as this sifting up of joy beneath all the comings and goings of everyday life. When I fall in love, which is fairly frequently, I can feel its sounds in my body like the vibrations of an ethereal bell making me sit up with longing.

I wonder if our evolution resides in the impulses of that profound instinct for love that persists in the world no matter what gets in its temporary way? Wars and violence, of course, but also the earth changes that last thousands of years—ice ages that lock whole continents under ice and snow; massive floods covering parts of the earth for millenia? Not once, but again and again.

We humans have persisted, haven't we? I wonder about those people, the animals and plants that lived and died in those days and nights uncountable—what did they learn from their lives? Do we carry their DNA and hold, in some fashion, their experiences?

Who were they, and who are we?

Who knows? But for better or for worse here we are, making one mistake after another and falling helplessly in love over and over again.

For each of us it all takes place for a meager handful of decades, while we learn whatever we can learn through every adventure imaginable, and when it's over we have to make way for the next generation to do the same. But even when we think it's over, I believe it is *not* over. The end of one phase transitions to the beginning of the next, and beneath it all—even when things look hopelessly bleak—the deep hope persists and the trend is ultimately toward the good.

We can lean towards one another and press our combined weight onto the ever-moving wheel of love. I believe we know how to do that, so why wait?

As Teilhard has said, "Deep hope flows over deep time."

And then,

There is an almost sensual longing for communion with others who have a large vision. The immense fulfillment of the friendship between those engaged in furthering the evolution of consciousness has a quality impossible to describe.

Yes, my dear love.

The only thing I would change is the word "almost" before the word "sensual."

Possible Impossibilities

for Darryl Berlin

At an open rehearsal of the LINES Ballet Company several years ago, I asked the choreographer, Alonzo King, if the dancers were free to improvise in performance.

"No," he replied, "the moves are all completely choreographed, although each dancer has a unique way of moving and flexibility is encouraged."

I've noticed, though, that over the years he has been using more improvisation in the training of his remarkable company, and I can see the difference. The choreography is still set, but the imaginative freedom with which these amazing artists dance has, in my eyes, become even more subtly expressive than before. It feels like their bodies are responding to a deeper beat, down where the hidden content of dreams resides. I reach for that in my own work, and I recognise the freedom of it when I see it.

In these times of breakdown and threat, I cannot imagine a technique more important for us all to learn, and to learn fast!

Albert Einstein once said that only those who attempt the absurd can achieve the impossible. He also said that creativity was intelligence having fun. I love that!

I watched intelligence having fun this week up at the farm, when my friends had an hour to get ready for a Halloween costume party but still hadn't figured out their costumes. Sara rooted up a corny old dress and an oversize blue wig, but Darryl was still lounging around the kitchen muttering something about the Wizard of Oz.

"At the end of the movie, don't they find him behind a green curtain?" he asked. Sara and I simply raised our eyebrows. He thought for awhile. "Do we have any green curtains around?"

I laughed at what I assumed was a joke.

"How are you planning to hold this curtain *up?*" I teased.

"We'll figure it out," he murmured, returning from the barn with a length of rubber tubing and some pieces of bamboo to create a round contraption to sit on top of his head. Cutting and twisting and drilling followed as I watched this ingenious structure take shape.

Sara came up with an old green curtain stashed in the back of some closet, I measured and cut it to size and made some holes for shower-curtain rings stolen from the bathroom.

Within a short hour Darryl was an invisible but chuckling Wizard of Oz hidden behind a round green curtain hanging from his head!

"They're going to guess you're a hotel shower," I commented to this apparition walking out the door a bit later.

"They did," he told me the next morning.

Attempting the absurd he achieved what had seemed to me impossible, it took less than an hour and we all had a blast in the process. Darryl was living proof that with a few basic skills and a wild imagination we can bring levity into even the most mundane of tasks, and make them work!

For example, I like to play at 'smoothies' in a game I call 'the DNA game.' You start with a banana and a slosh of almond milk and get a bland white mixture—sort of Western European—but add a touch of maple syrup to it and you can imagine some hanky-panky way back between a native Cherokee, say, and an early White colonizer.

Then pour in a cup of orange juice and the mixture gets sort of ruddy—Middle Eastern, maybe? A bit of applesauce adds tones of yellow and you've got Asian and Indian; a handful of berries, and the mixture could be, maybe, Mongolian. A dollop of peanut butter for protein adds light brown—Philippino—and almond butter makes it a bit darker and you've got Mayan, North African. Darken it still more with squares of chocolate and cocoa powder and you've got the whole African continent!

Delicious!

All it takes is a good blender—and over the generations we sexy humans have been *very* good blenders!

I giggle and my taste buds register the spicy sweetness; my heart registers a new feeling; my soul recognizes the possibilities inherent in a multicultural world. How much fun is *that?*

It's happening more and more when I walk out my door; I cross paths with Sonan, a Tibetan who lives around the corner and Asok, a Bengali who lives across the street from him. I walk up the block with Kerry, our African-American mailman on my way to Susanna's place—Susanna, who is half Chinese, and grew up in China during the Cultural Revolution.

I stop to chat with Michiko who was born in Tokyo on exactly the same day my husband Herb was born in Germany, and then go into our neighborhood grocery where Sidi, the grocer I've known for years, confesses he always wanted to be a Math professor and go back to Palestine.

It's all a big improvisation, learning how to live in our constantly evolving smoothie—I mean, *world.*

My brother, a farmer in Vermont, is even more of an improviser than I am. For example, if I take scraps of cloth found here and there to sew patchwork quilts, he gathers scraps of wood and turns them into *buildings!*

Well, sheds, he'd say. My favorite one is the sugaring shed behind their farmhouse at the edge of a field, close to one of the maples they tap for sap. The shed is little more than three walls and a metal roof, but as he will tell you proudly, "There's not one right angle in the place!" He reworks it every year, shoring it up after a winter of snow loads, hammering new pieces in here and there as cunningly as you please.

For decades it has been an ongoing artwork which he likens to a newborn foal learning how to stand up straight, listing a little to the right, then to the left until it finds its center of gravity—for this year, at least.

"It's good for another hundred years, easy," he tells me with a grin.

I've been around during sugaring season many a year when the sap gets boiled down in sawed-off metal tubs over roaring fires of scrap wood that burn night and day for as long as the sap is running. Normally, snow is still on the ground and the nights are clear and cold, but it is warm in the shed as fragrant steam softens the air and there you are, standing in an impressionist movie of all the senses, totally happy. An extension cord from the house provides all the light you need to keep stirring and pouring the thickening syrup, tasting (of course) and, if kids are present, dripping a filled ladle onto a patch of clean snow for popsicles.

That's what I call *living*, and in my heart of hearts I know it can save us.

Getting simple. Making it up. Having a good time with your neighbors while doing what you need to do.

Really, making little holes in a tree so it drips its nutritious sap? Whoever dreamed up such an absurd notion, and made the impossible possible?

Who? The Native peoples who would have starved by the end of winter had they had not found an unlikely source of nutrition—that's who!

Oh

This just arrived in my inbox from Adebayo Akomolafe, a Nigerian poet who lives with his Indian wife and children in Chenai, India, which is now under floodwaters:

"When our hearts break, that is how they intend to accommodate more space—more room for the impossible."

May it be so, and may he and his family be safe.

Diverse Blessings

in memoriam, Burton Heda, M.D.

Down at the Bay early this morning, the duck congregation was out on the water—buffleheads and grebes, canvasbacks and ruddy ducks—their many-colored plumage reflecting bright on calm water as they drifted by.

The walkers and joggers were out too, equally colorful in magenta shorts and orange headbands, *hijabs* and *burqas*. One young woman, in full headdress and skirts down to her shoes, greeted me with a bright "Good morning" as she jogged past, going at a good clip even in her full skirts.

Our morning had already been dramatic, with a fire in the hills and a bus careening into a house in the flats, but the peaceable scene of diverse life down by the Bay reassured me; we'll make it through, I kept thinking, we'll make it through. It was the diversity of ducks drifting together on placid water, and the Muslim woman jogging on the path that calmed my soul.

My ideal neighborhood is a mélange of languages and skin colors, and, having grown up unhappy in an all-white suburb of New York City, I am happiest when surrounded by a multiplicity, as it mostly is down by the Bay.

That may be why I had such a good time, in the mid-1960s, volunteering in the Emergency Room of Herrick Hospital where people of every color and language eventually found their way through those swishing double doors.

My first day there, a Phillipina staggered in on the arms of her husband and was attended by a Russian-Jewish doctor, an African-American nurse and a Chinese orderly—with me in the mix. I felt I was where I belonged.

I was there in the ER, having the opportunity of a lifetime being trained in preparation for a year in India where Herb would teach at a local college and I would be a kind of 'barefoot nurse' in the surrounding villages. Our family doctor graciously invited me into the Emergency Room as a volunteer during his shifts, so he could show me the basic 'ropes.' I would learn from him mostly by watching him work and asking questions about what I observed, and it was not long before others on staff were also training me, even allowing me to assist in small ways.

Most important, though, I was learning to keep cool in the face of pain and fear, and to not faint at the sight of blood.

"A little blood goes a long way," Nurse Sara pointed out, wiping gore off the face of a young guy thrown from his motorcycle, and showing me the small nick under his hairline where all that blood was coming from. "Lots of blood vessels in the scalp," she explained, applying pressure.

Like that, I learned.

One evening, while we had a quiet moment in the nurses' station, a baby was brought in screaming and I watched the doctor go still, calmly pop another jellybean into his mouth and then saunter off to the examining room to see the baby. I was as frantic as the mother, wanting to yell at him to get a move on! When I scolded him afterwards, he smiled and said, "He was hollering like all get-out, right?"

I nodded.

"That was the sound of a healthy baby. If he'd been silent, I would have run."

"Stay calm until it is time to be busy; do not waste good energy getting emotional," was that day's lesson.

That year in the ER was an invaluable education—at least as significant as the experience of India itself—and taught me just how resilient the human body and spirit can be, how I could rise to the occasion when I had to, and how essential was human kindness in the process of healing.

That doctor, Burt Heda, and his family were like family to us for years, and now both he and Herb are gone. It is the end of an era. Yesterday, I received a package from their daughter containing letters to her parents I'd written from India about my medical adventures there. The family had kept them!

My early letters were a litany of complaints: I hated the caste system, the oppressive heat; the poverty. The local hospital had cows wandering in the corridors and every little rash became septic! My attempts to inoculate the servants' children against rampant tuberculosis didn't work because we couldn't get the serum, and yesterday I delivered the baby of a malnourished fourteen year old!

It took months of fuming before I settled down and learned to let go of my judgments, my privilege and expectations and go with what was right in front of me. It felt like letting a cloak slip quietly off my shoulders, leaving me naked and vulnerable to a different reality than I was used to. Hard lesson, and it took me most of a year to learn.

What really woke me up was what happened after the delivery of a servant's baby during monsoon season. After I had examined the newborn, tied the umbilical cord (with a shoelace!) and delivered the afterbirth, I handed him to his young mother and went out to tell his father the 'good' news. A boy!

(A daughter, in fact, might *not* have been good news.)

Next morning I came back to check on mother and child, and found the baby's body covered in what looked like excrement! Horrified, I told them to wash off the baby right away! The women looked frightened, and shook their heads. The next day, the baby was still covered in goo—this time with a knife lying by his little head as well—and his eyes were outlined in black kohl. Again, I took charge and showed them how to wash the baby until every bit of goo was cleansed from his tender skin.

On the third day they finally obeyed me, the *memsahib*, and when I returned the next morning the baby was covered with red welts from mosquito bites! O God! Of course! The crushed mustard seed covering, the traditional protection from the prevalent and dangerous mosquitos had been completely washed off—at my insistence!

In that moment, I grew up, hard. Ever since, I try and opt for humility about what I think I know!

"Separate perspectives are merely different facets of the same perfect diamond," writes Dr. Eben Alexander, the neurosurgeon who 'died' and came back from his near-death experience to report that reality was more vast, more dimensioned and more loving than we have been taught.

"We live in a many-faceted, many-dimensioned, interconnected, conscious universe, and belong to it all," he reports back. Every one of us, every particle through all time and space is part of the Whole. No matter what it looks like nor how it communicates to every other part, its language is beauty and its message is love.

The material world is just a layer, after all—a beautiful layer, to be sure, but really only a congealed crust of the infinite Whole, and is actually minimal in comparison to the Whole Picture. Without the Whole, nothing we see would even exist.

Nor would we.

Down at the Bay, just as I was leaving, a great blue heron alighted in all its feathered glory, posing itself like a gorgeous sculpture by the water, still and gleaming in the morning sunshine.

I stopped, stood still, and stared.

To Be or Not To Be

for Jak Noble

This bug making its way around town is a persistent one—as soon as the cough simmers down, the nausea starts in and when that's over, it's sore throat time. It's been a month of this smorgasbord, sapping my strength for everything but naps and Irish novels. I'm slowing way down to an enforced stillness and noticing the wisdom in this; it's like a meditation in which I am aware of every little thing, especially my own short human life on earth.

It is frightening to look too closely because for myself and everyone alive in the world right now, 'every little thing' includes so much that is horrific and more dire than we can imagine, and much we dare not even begin to imagine.

But then, has there ever been a generation for whom poverty and war, greed and violence have *not* been the case?

For example, I was born into refugee poverty and my family history includes suicides and pogroms, deaths of our young men in war, murder and paralysis, incest and child abuse. I was the kid who kept to herself and dreamed of green mountains and shining lakes, ashamed of the rough people I belonged to.

I've always suspected myself of the Pollyanna syndrome, dreaming up a fantasies of goodness to cover up my actual soul sickness, hiding from the truth of myself as well as the truth of my world—a kid in denial, pretending to be who she wished to be, but wasn't. Now, in my mature years and with the help of a skilled healer, I want to dig deep into the truth of myself, and discover the authentic ground of my being.

"You're down in close, but you don't need to dig in rock!" warned Jak seriously, "Brush away at the loose sand and mud and let it get washed away by your life force, like a river. But be very careful!"

So I dug in rock—of course—and that night choked myself awake from a nightmare in which I couldn't breathe. In the dream, stuck in the airless cabin of a grounded airplane, I was ready to let go of life, but then found myself half-awake and sucking it back in, breath by body-shaking breath. I can still feel that struggle against the fog, my chest heaving as the dark closed in.

But in those moments of gasping for breath something came clear and I got it, perhaps for the first time, that my creative personality was *not* just a defense against despair, it was who I was! That I actually am by nature a positive spirit! I woke all the way up, gulping in real air and sitting up against the headboard, knowing myself to be authentic—not a sham.

I was someone I could trust!

Jak, I had to finally know this; that's why I dug into the rock.

I fell back to sleep, reassured after all these years of wondering if I was or was not an imposter.

I'm not. Neither are any of you, I'll bet.

I can never forget the heartbreaking night—I was about seven—when the whole world was celebrating the Armistice of World War II and "the boys were coming home!"

In our house, though, there was only keening because Leon, my mother's beloved twenty-two year old brother, would *not* be coming home.

Instead of him, we got a 'Purple Heart' in a box in the mail.

That night of helpless wailing, I believe, was when my mother finally cracked. One by one we all did, I think.

Our family disintegrated after that, and given that every generation in human history, it seems, goes through its own version of wars and tragic loss, is it any wonder that we collectively suffer from depression and self-doubt, the misery being passed down from mothers and fathers to their children, *ad infinitum?*

We are links in a chain of sorrow.

I had a dream that night that is as clear to me now as it was at the end of the war when I was seven and my uncle did not come back from the war with 'the boys.'

> *"I have come to a New York City tenement building, and I go up the stairs and down a dark hallway looking at the numbers on each door. One door is partly open and I look in, but instead of an apartment, there is a cathedral—forbidden ground for little Jewish girls like me. This is Hitler time. But something draws me into that long, dark space—a choir singing at the altar—and I walk down the long nave towards the music. I belong here. Robed singers embrace me with welcome, their voices reaching into my sadness. They sing and sing, and rock me. I want to stay, but I cannot. With their eyes they let me know that even though I have to leave, I can return.*
>
> *"Just look for the slightly open door—anywhere."*

Years later, I would make a study of 12th century cathedrals, looking for that one! Indeed, I found it again and again in different guises all over France where he had been killed. In each one I felt taken in and comforted.

As I move into the last decades of my life I know, more and more, that it is indeed authentic beauty that redeems us, no matter what madness of war and greed is being perpetrated out there. We can love one another despite this and create the positive beauty that we know how to do, no matter how we do it.

Many are the ways of artistry and loving. Many are the authentic tools for creation, and we've all got them, no matter how much we've covered them over with protective polish.

We're the real thing.

Trust me—we can trust ourselves.

Fun at the Races

I'm stuck! I just learned that both my wonderful nephew and my beloved grandson, who live in different states, have inadvertently scheduled their weddings on the same day!

What to do?

The fact is I have no idea: one is the son of my son, the other the son of my brother! How can I possibly make a choice?

I'll figure it out because I have to, but I am dismayed that the family was not consulted in the first place! Didn't we count?

It reminds me of how people of color must feel as the laws of the land and the mindset of the white majority assumes its own privilege, and tends not to consider others. It is not only unjust, it's also *stupid* because the people who call the shots—the dominant culture—is unaware of how much they're missing!

Years ago, when I sang in the Gospel Choir of an African-American church, we had a choir retreat on the Delta, away from the city lights. By that time, I'd been part of the church family for a few years and could (sort of) hold my own playing 'the dozens' with the best of them. To be part of that congregation—White Jewish woman that I was—was a profound privilege for me, as I experienced an ecstasy so rich and deep, it brought me to my knees.

One memorable night at the retreat, outside under the full moon, we raised our voices in praise—up and up towards the heavens—sharing knowledge of the Ineffable together, singing our way in praise— Glory Hallelujah!

They called it Jesus. For me, it was nameless. White folks have no idea what they are missing.

I believe it is what we all long for, though, this feeling of belonging to one another and to the cosmos—whether we know it or not.

Geneticists point out that human DNA, across the spectrum of ethnicities and cultures, lifestyles and geography, is 95% identical. The last tiny percentage contains the differences of bone structure, eye shape and skin color—just the finishing touches of what we look like.

So what's this big deal we've managed to create? As one geneticist put it, "Skin color should be the last nail in the coffin for racism."

How in hell do we heal this rift?

I went, this week, to see some dance films at the LINES Ballet Center where Alonzo King has been encouraging members of the general community to come and take dance classes—*everyone!* There are classes for the little ones and the pre-teens, for working mothers and fathers, for retired or crippled folks, for the young bloods.

In the introductory film, I was captivated by one little girl in the children's class, maybe five years old, with brown skin and bright, black eyes, who raised her arms rapturously to the music while her many-colored classmates swayed around her. In another scene young boys with lots of hair hip-hopped through their wild moves, their faces intense and shining; and in another a middle-aged white man spoke of finally getting to dance after a lifetime of wishing to.

I sat there crying. This is the world I wish to live in. How did we get so off track?

This social dilemma of ours is not only about righting a history of abuse, it is about all of us losing out on the privilege of knowing one another and the extraordinary riches each of us brings to the table.

I cannot imagine living my life without Shadi's warm and exotic personality, not to mention her Persian cooking. Have you ever sat still while a nine year-old Filipina drew a picture of you and it *looked* like you?

I watch the ones coming of age now, falling in love with one another across every line of color and culture, creating the most gorgeous babies I've ever seen. These are our new grown-ups, may they thrive! I met one lovely young woman recently who I couldn't place racially, and asked about her background.

"Oh, my Mom's from Colombia and my Dad's Punjabi," she replied. I tried to imagine what a man from the Punjab was doing in South America, or a Colombian woman doing in India?

"However did they meet?" I asked.

"At work," she said, it being the most natural thing in the world.

I had to laugh. This was America at the turn of the 21st century, and even with all its burps and warts, why shouldn't people who immigrated here from everywhere in the world meet at work? And fall in love, and create the new generation of bright and beautiful beings like this young woman, mixing up the gene pool in yet another ingenious way!

We should not be surprised! It's true, our country is in a big fat mess, but I'm not ready to give up on it. My hope is that if I just stick with it through *its* labor pains, it might stick with me through *mine*.

And labor, as we know, can hurt like the devil and rarely goes quickly, but I've never known a woman to change her mind in the middle.

Have you?

We're All in this Mess Together

for Roger Nelson

Last week, glued to the screen watching the Royal wedding and then the new film about Pope Francis, I realized that millions of people around the world were focusing on both these events along with me! Together, our collective energy field was being raised by positive emotion as we witnessed both a biracial royal marriage, and the welcoming of a well-loved Pope.

Whatever we may think about either Monarchy or The Church, the fact is that each is followed passionately by millions of people. This has to generate a spurt of heightened energy on the global airwaves!

According to Roger Nelson, who runs the Global Consciousness Project, this has a real-time effect on all of us because at the level of our neurons we are subtly interconnected, like cells in a single organism. It follows, then, that if groups of people respond to anything with joy and excitement, they are raising the vibrational frequency of their own bodies as well as everyone else's on the planet. The greater the joy, the higher the frequency—just as hatred and violence *lowers* the frequencies of all our bodies.

As Roger says,

The more we understand we're all One, as the sages of all cultures put it, the better able we'll be to shift our activities to realize our huge, wonderful potential. Without a course change, we may not have a future at all.

As it happened, I heard from Roger that same week—synchronicity at work!—and we agreed that the royal wedding and the Pope in the movies were indeed significant signs of course change.

At this point, it might be too late to make this course change gracefully, but what if it could be done *ungracefully*—just so long as we *did* it?

I had an unwelcome chance to try that out recently, when I was stood up two days in a row by a friend I had looked forward to seeing. Feeling forgotten and hurt, I huffed around for a day of self-pity before realizing this was a chance to get out some hard emotions that have been needing expression for a long time, so I went for it.

Out came my helpless anxiety about melting glaciers and depleted soil, and the horrors of immigrants being shoved out of this country. I moaned about greedy bankers and puerile politicians, at narrow-minded scientists and racist idiots, and the fact that I no longer hear birds calling in the morning. That made me curl up on the floor sobbing. Tears flowed for the children of all species struggling to survive in this Silent Spring, and the waters sullied with plastic. Then I went after my misguided father who looked for love in the wrong places and my mother who tried not to see it—and then my own guilt at not being able to save either of them.

Anybody passing by would have witnessed a wild woman yelling at the walls, but I just went for it, down on my knees with slam and be-damn and who cares if someone thinks I'm crazy?

I made a good old mess of the house, and after an hour or two was tired of my rantings, but it had been just what I'd needed. The fact is that without the goad I never would have gone there.

So thanks, buddy—sort of.

Glancing at my calendar the next morning, I was chastened to see that I had inadvertently stood up someone *else* while I was ranting and raving! I tripped all over my own feet apologizing and we laughed together until we cried.

The reality is that so many of us are on edge these days with so many fears, and we know that fear, like laughter and kindness, is contagious. As Roger says, all of life is intrinsically interconnected and what happens to any one being happens simultaneously to *all other* beings for we are a single organism made up of multiple parts, and siblings of the same Mother Earth.

Separation is nothing but an illusion.

I had a visceral experience of this when I was about five years old and was taken to see Walt Disney's "Bambi" at Radio City Music Hall in New York City. A very special treat! An impressionable little kid, I identified with all the little animals, especially Bambi, of course, and in the scene where his mother is shot and killed by a hunter I had hysterics, losing my breath and choking in helpless grief. They had to rush me out of the theater, and I can still feel those helpless screams coming out of my small body, as the realities of the world poured in on me: I *was* Bambi, I *was* his dead mother, I *was* the hunter.

Bambi taught me, at five, that we were all in this together. I didn't know then about my neurons being interconnected with all living beings, but clearly I got that we were all in the boat together no matter what or who we were, no matter what we looked like, or what we did.

Roger, I wonder how long this course change is likely to take?

I'm reminded of those wonderful children's books—which I still read and reread when I need inspiration—in which eleven year-olds, often girls, take on the forces of Darkness, always unwittingly, and eventually, after many dangerous adventures, their innocent courage releases the forces of Light back into the world!

In my favorite books it is only on the very last page that danger is finally averted and goodness prevails. *Only* when everything seems lost does this happen.

That gives me hope. I wonder if that is where we collectively are now—on that last page, quivering in shock right at the very center of the labyrinth? And if so, what do we do now?

Personally, I think we could start by breathing, and then remember that we do not have to do this alone because we are all in this together.

All!

No exceptions.

Shifting Consciousness

for G.S. Sachdev, in memoriam

In the 1960s, when Timothy Leary was exhorting kids my age to turn on, tune in and drop out, the psychologist Frank Barron and I found one another in the crowd and became secret collaborators. I was curious about his research on creativity and how psychedelics affected artists, and he was interested in people, like me, who had access to these 'psychedelic' states without the use of drugs.

For about a year we met in his office on campus for clandestine conversations—very cloak and dagger—with me slipping in after-hours when his colleagues were gone, to compare notes. I loved it! Nobody knew what we were up to—maybe we didn't either—but what we did together confirmed for me that I wasn't crazy. Psychedelic substances apparently were helping people to see a wider reality, because most people seemed trapped in the 'rational' mindset of our culture that was keeping so many of us frightened and depressed.

I intuitively saw another kind of reality, much larger than what we were taught at school, in which the world was a miraculous, positive and joyous place of many dimensions, a place of challenge and adventure, not meant to be a vale of tears where everyone was afraid of their own shadows.

When did we get talked into that?

I felt strongly about this, even then, because we were clearly lost as a society, with racism and wars rampant everywhere. I felt sure that if people could experience firsthand the ecstatic wonder of this universe, we'd be able to shift the collective zeitgeist from angst and fear to a more positive, even joyous vision of what was real.

As one volunteer in the NYU psilocybin trials, as I read it in Michael Pollan's new book *How To Change Your Mind* put it, "if everyone had this experience, no one could ever do harm to one another again—wars would be impossible to wage."

What Frank and I were each confirming in our own ways was essentially this: that the universe was infinite in all dimensions, and that every particle within it was in motion—dancing—with everything else, all interconnected on every level of Being through Time and Space and beyond. And that everything in this 'soup of Being' was beautiful and conscious—indeed, was Consciousness itself—and underlying the whole thing, like cosmic glue, was Love.

It was all ultimately about Love, delicious love. So utterly beautiful … then Frank and I gazed at one another and blushed.

This memory is very poignant for me right now, as G.S. Sachdev, my beloved longtime friend since we first met in India in the late sixties, died this week.

It was some kind of magic that brought us together that day. As Herb and I wandered the streets of Old Delhi, we heard someone playing the flute outdoors, and it sounded rich and deep as if there was such a thing as a bass bamboo flute! Of all things! We took off towards the sound until, in a small courtyard between two alleys, we found a fellow in flowing white, cross-legged on a string cot playing some of the most gorgeous music I had ever heard in my life. On a bass bamboo flute!

Maybe there are no accidents, that we were meant to meet but the rest is history—fifty years worth of history. We became friends and then, well—relatives. On the Sikh holiday when brothers and sisters pledge their devotion by tying bracelets of jasmine around one another's wrists, we became sister and brother and have kept our promise all these years, first in India and then in California.

Oddly, we look enough alike that we were often mistaken for siblings anyhow, but from the first time I heard him play his bamboo flute on that day in Old Delhi, I knew he was one of my 'clan.'

What I remember of that day was being spellbound by both the music I was hearing and what I was feeling. His notes poured into the air like smoke spiraling from a candle, shifting depth and timbre as they morphed into variations of themselves with his breath. I shivered, and the hairs on my arms stood up. My whole body felt carried by sound into spaciousness where everything is Light. I recognized this as a mystical state, where sound becomes color becomes taste becomes love, a world in perfect balance even in the midst of a city bathed in tropical heat, where whole families lived on the streets.

Two years later, as the world music scene began to flourish in the Bay Area, Herb and I helped to bring him and his family to America where he introduced the Bansuri, the bass bamboo flute, to a whole new generation of young American musicians, and we became 'family' again on the other side of the world.

He started his own school here and eventually played and taught all over the world, recording many of his concerts so that, although he himself is no longer amongst us, his music continues to live on. We need it more than ever now, to be reminded that our lives take place in a conscious universe and that we were built for ecstatic wonder, not sorrow.

Life is a miracle, nothing less, and we can wake up to it at any moment, singly and together. When enough of us have evolved to a state of heightened consciousness, however we get there, the Frumps and the Plumps will be left behind in the dust.

On good days, I can feel some gratitude that we are being pushed to wake up and see the world in new ways, because the old ways are over and are hanging on like the tangled hairs that get stuck in the bathtub drain. 'Chaos bundles,' Jak calls them. Yuck. We can clean them up—and gag at the muck—but fresh water is available and even if it takes several scrubbings to clean up the place, we can do that.

Sachdev will be cremated tomorrow, completing this cycle after a remarkable life on earth.

I recall asking him one night, after a concert when his whole body glowed with warm light from his own playing,

"How do you prepare, time after time, to touch us all so deeply?" He thought for a moment, then said softly,

"I don't prepare. I just play the flute."

Crisis into Adventure
for Joanna Macy

This morning, idly reminiscing about the time I was a student in France, I recalled my bus trip to the village of Chars, north of Paris, when I thought I was going to visit the cathedral in Chartres, south of Paris!

As I got off the bus, I asked the driver to point me towards the Cathedral. Chars was the last on his line, more village than town, with no cathedral in sight.

He told me about the nice little church there, *la bas*, but no cathedral, and he shrugged apologetically. I insisted, he shrugged, led me into the café where we finally untangled the story to the great laughter and kindness of the good folk of Chars, who put me up for the night, fed me and laughed uproariously at my mistake.

It wouldn't surprise me if I am still part of the town's folklore.

Two days later, and many hours of traveling in the other direction, I found myself at last in Chartres where, in the famous Cathedral, I met one of the great loves of my life. My crisis had, in fact, been perfectly timed.

These unexpected synchronicities happen to me frequently, and I live by them. I never know what will come from what. Bad news turns into good news, mistakes turn into opportunities, the hardest times become the biggest teachers.

I think our current political situation can be one of those hard times we can use that way, if we choose to, although it may not be easy and I expect will take much courage and imagination on our parts, but I am not sure we have a choice. This is make-or-break time and it may go on for quite awhile and, speaking for myself, I will not let this administration break me! We're being prodded to change, rethink our priorities and use the pressure as a test of our imaginations and grit. And our ability to keep the love going without giving in to fear, nor reciprocal hatred, no matter what!

It's either all of us coming through these times, I believe, or none of us.

Yes, what is happening is terrifying and horrific, cruel and unbelievable, but I see us gathering collective steam, and more and more of us know we have to do this together. We've been kicked in the pants—hard—but I'm seeing us, the young ones especially, teaming up and brilliantly dreaming up the new world, and it is time! My wish is to help them accomplish it, and to live in that world with them.

They seem to understand that the work is *not* about trying to find our way back to a barely working system that has been unjust and imperfect for far too long already. They are choosing to reimagine an interrelated world on a balanced, healthy Earth in which love and respect, rather than conflict and profit form the template.

They are smart, these young ones, and energetic, and it's more than time that we listen to what they are saying—they and the indigenous elders they are learning from.

The other day I went out to the Wild and Radish Farm, where I will probably be living in the next year or so, and as I arrived I saw that Maisie, one of the Mama goats, was in labor.

Oh my! Shuddering moans and heaving of flanks, and from her opening, a pointy nose and tiny hooves pushing its way out, until a whole baby goat plopped wetly onto the ground, and took in its first breath!

I didn't know what to do first—get towels? Call someone? But while I deliberated, there came another one, nose first, surprising even Maisie, who stepped on her firstborn in confusion, not knowing which baby to lick first. It was hilarious! So she went back and forth between them, trying to lick them both dry while the twins staggered to their feet and boldly took off in opposite directions.

It was clear what I had to do, and I did it: corralling the kids, keeping Maisie's hooves off them, squeezing her teats to get milk flowing, helping both babies find those teats, wiping everyone off, staying out the way of hanging strings of bloody afterbirth, and crooning congratulations as Maisie burbled burp—like sounds to her kidlets and they reported back with *beh-beh-behs,* sucking lustily as they were welcomed into our world.

Instinctively, we all knew what to do.

We humans know what to do, also. We may think we don't because it's all become so complicated, but we do. We just have to keep our wits about us, trust in our instincts, know we are encoded with knowledge we may not even be aware we have, and realize we are all in this together with love as our base root reality.

And to hold our ground against destructive forces that would take over our humanity with force! No, no! We have to resist with tough love in the face of the Darkness, no matter what!

After all, taking the wrong bus happens, no big deal, and it can be an opportunity to see some new places, have a good laugh at ourselves and meet some good people we would never have otherwise met. We might even find one of the loves of our life there, or have a chance to give comfort where we least expected to.

The wild ride is on, folks, and we're in it. Hang onto your hats, open your hearts wide, hold hands with the rest of us and keep your sense of humor handy!

We'll need it.

Friendship

for Taylor and Brighid

I stood in the Security line at the airport behind a Buddhist monk from Thailand, and watched helplessly as the agents roughed him up, opening his bags and tossing the contents onto the floor. They were probably following orders to harass people who looked 'foreign.' I helped him gather up his things and move them out of the way of passengers following close behind, saying over and over to him, "I'm sorry, I'm so sorry."

When I handed him his sneakers, both of us were close to tears. He put his palms together and bowed, whispering, *"Gassho."*

I stayed with him until he was again in his ocher robes, the yellow rope tied around his middle, his bags well closed and we had shared several bows. *Gassho* was whispered with each bow, and I kept repeating, "I'm so sorry," and then he spoke in perfectly good English with the hint of a grin, "It's alright—this how I make a friend!" We both laughed, and then had one last bow before he hurried off to make his plane and I hurried off to make mine.

I have been thinking about friendship ever since, and how much we need good friends by our sides when the times get rough, which they are doing right now. Facing the world alone when we're frightened is too sad to contemplate. I realized this so poignantly after my husband—who was also my best friend and companion—died. I missed him achingly: the presence of him, the daily support of him, the very maleness of his body. I found myself talking to him for company, telling the walls things I told nobody else. To anybody passing by, I would have been a crazy lady.

About five months after his death I found myself at a gathering I really didn't want to go to and a young man approached me and said simply, "I want to know you." His candor was so refreshing, like a shock of warm water that I responded by asking him, "Why?"

"I'm not sure," he replied with the blunt innocence I have come to love and count on in him, "but I have a feeling that you know something I need to learn." I probably smiled and asked, "What is that?" He shrugged and then changed the subject.

As I am much older than he, I assumed he did this kind of thing for a lark, and we eventually drifted to other people in the room. But I was wrong; he meant it, and now almost four years later we are bonded by a committed friendship so real and honest it has helped me through my long period of grief.

He may never know how much.

The fact is that we are fascinated by many of the same things, which he apparently intuited that night, and now we talk about them all, from the nature of reality to the effects of music and sound on the soul. We explore questions of intimacy and mutual commitment, marriage and non-sexual expressions of love.

His remarkable (and remarkably patient) wife joins us from time to time, apparently bemused by her open-hearted husband's friendship with this older woman who seems to share his penchant for digging into the roots of human relationships. I'd love to know her and their young-adult children as well as I know him, though I wouldn't be surprised if, behind our backs, she rolls her eyes at our antics.

Who we are to one another is an ongoing question, and we seek out answers by wandering the North Coast sea cliffs and talking non-stop, and trekking in the woods to waterfalls where we contemplate falling water that is ever changing and ever the same. Yesterday we took a picnic right to the edge of the surf and plopped down, not knowing if the tide was going in or out, while pelicans appeared by the dozens to fly over us as if in celebration of our daring.

We have cried together over the horrors in our world, and have flown kites in the wind until we were weak with laughter. We contemplate the possible and the impossible, and then prepare to do both.

I am fortunate that we met at this gathering he almost did not come to and I was not in the mood for, because grieving alone makes people crazy and is more painful than we know. I believe that is why widows traditionally wear black—to signal to others to give them a little space to be nuts, without censure.

Anyhow, I suspect we are all, consciously or unconsciously, grieving now. Or should be.

Please, be careful.

We are all in this time of fear and trembling together and we need to have our friends to cherish and be cherished by. We need to love and to be loved, to not be alone when the sweeping storms of the world threaten to engulf us, because the storms are already howling and more are coming.

We need to find and create community with at least one other person who knows us, accepts us and trusts us no matter what. Under duress, we have to be there for one another because survival in community may be the only way we can make it through these times. Nobody ever said it would be easy, but there you are: together, or not at all.

As Taylor said to me that first evening, "I want to know you."

And as the Thai monk said after being deeply insulted by the airport Security agents, "It is alright—this is how I make a friend."

Gassho.

Soul Dance

These days, as I delve deep into my past, I remember …

At 15, I was longing to dance but my parents would not permit it. Why? I suspect it was fear; they were from the "don't run, you'll fall; don't swim, you'll drown" generation. So I secretly applied for a summer job in the kitchen of a music and dance camp in the mountains so I could dance when I wasn't washing dishes. The teacher was someone I'd seen perform, a tall, supple man named Donald McKayle who seemed to belong to both earth and air, grounded but able to fly, which is what I longed to do. It was daring for me to apply—either for the kitchen job or as a student—so I kept it from my parents; I especially kept from them that this man was "a Negro."

I knew quality when I saw it, and he was quality—body, mind and spirit. For ten full weeks he would be teaching at Deerwood, a music and dance camp in the Adirondack Mountains, and even if I only got to sit in on the occasional class between meals, it was worth it to me, so I showed up for the job interview to work in the kitchen.

"Why don't you just apply as a student?" the Director asked reasonably. I think I mumbled, "My parents won't let me …" and then my whole story poured out. He stamped his foot angrily, accepted me as a full-time student and said he would come to my house and talk to them. "Where do you live? Don't tell them I'm coming, but make sure they are home on Sunday at 11, okay?"

And there he was, exactly on time, a stranger at the door on a mission. My parents were shocked, to say the least, and when he said, "Do you know your daughter offered to work in our kitchen so that she could study dance?" They all but hung their heads.

After that, they could hardly say No.

Once there, in the fragrant Adirondack woods on the shores of Saranac Lake, my body woke up to being danced several hours a day—ballet, modern, African—even though I was a beginner in classes with experienced dancers my own age. I tried not to act humiliated (even though I was) and worked hard to learn quickly. Donald was kind, no doubt knowing full well how it felt to not belong, and I never missed a single class.

In off hours we were introduced to ethnic dance, from Indian *mudras* to African polyrhythms, and in this I did well as my body took to the indigenous rhythms easily. Astonishing myself and finding where I belonged I came alive, and soared! Every day I blessed my opportunity to learn from this man, and I shudder to think what I might have missed had I obeyed my frightened parents.

Donny and the kitchen staff were the only people of color at Deerwood, and I liked to help out in the kitchen after meals and hang with them, but it was not encouraged. When a cello student fell in love with one of the kitchen staff it caused a current of ruckus all over camp until Donny smoothed things over, and they became more discreet; but everyone was more careful after that, and any such liaisons went underground.

Love, in that gorgeous place surrounded by lakes and mountains with music in the air night and day was, of course, everywhere and the students began to pair off by the second week. One violin player in the orchestra fixed his sights on me, but he wasn't my type, and anyhow I needed to stay focused on learning the complicated moves of Martha Graham technique. John was flatteringly persistent and quite good looking, but I was there to dance! I figured that once the summer was over he would settle into college life anyway—he'd been accepted at Harvard—so for the summer we could just be friends.

I tell this story because it took another three years for him to finally let go, and it took going to one of Donny's performances in the city together for both of us to understand why.

John and I went to see a production of "Games," an early work based on children's sidewalk games in the streets of New York's tenement neighborhoods. Marbles and Ringolevio, Mother-May-I? and chasing games are all played out onstage until one boy calls out, "Chickee, the cops!" And the children scatter out of sight, all but one who runs back to retrieve a ball. A shot rings out, the boy falls, the stage grows dim, the songs go silent and the curtain falls on the spotlighted boy lying dead in the street.

I fell apart. Sobbing uncontrollably, I collapsed into John's arms and repeated over and over, "I want to be good!"

I will never forget the moment of finally knowing that.

"And you think you can't be good with me, is that it?" he asked sadly, edging me away from the crowd. The only honest answer I could give him was a nod of the head "yes." I finally understood what was missing between us, the very same thing that was there for me with Donny. I had no name for it then, but now I would call it Soul.' It was a sense of deep family, of belonging to a world that encompassed everything, not only the obvious stuff. It was what I felt when I danced, that I could never express in words.

John was brilliant, but he had no idea what I was talking about, and perhaps it was that very quality of 'knowing' in me that attracted him to me. It took me three years to understand that I was not responsible for giving him—or anyone—something of myself that was too subtle to even name, unless I chose to or knew how to. Especially as I didn't really understand what that feeling was! I just felt it.

Whatever it was, I had recognized it in Donny the first time I saw him dance, and it was only much later that I could put a name to it:

Soul.

Thank you, Donny, for that life-changing production of "Games" that broke my heart, gave me my freedom, and clarified my mind. It also, by instilling my passion for racial justice, made me understand just what we white folks were missing by not knowing people from the cultures of the African diaspora.

Thank you, my friend and teacher for showing me your language of the body in motion—in beautiful motion—and for your soul that went deep and embraced me. Oh, if only white folks understood that what you carry is what we are desperate for, but are terrified of. Actually, we may understand it perfectly well, but reject it because of its power! That may be the scariest thing of all.

During his long and successful career, Donald McKayle used his art form like brass knuckles in a velvet glove. It packed a wallop while it opened hearts to a shared humanity, despite the history of abduction and slavery, despite torture and shaming, lynching and deprivation.

For over half a century, his work bore witness to survival under great odds, and inherent genius in the face of racism and slavery. Donny used dance and music to move the soul, to tell the Black story—the human story—showcasing the ritual and art forms of the African diaspora. He was truly a jewel in our midst; some now might say he was an extraterrestrial, for surely his energy and his output were larger than earth-life!

I ran into him only one more time, half a century later, in California where he was teaching a Master Class in the Gym at Cal. Half the students were people of color, and the combinations he taught were even more complex than the ones I once had to learn, but the students did just fine. It was all so familiar, and yet so very different. The world had changed.

I sat in the bleachers watching, wondering if I should go up and greet him when class was over. I stayed for awhile afterwards as the crowd descended upon him, and then I left the gym slowly, wondering if he would notice me and look my way. I doubt he did.

In any case, of course he would not remember me. The past was almost half a century before, and gone. I knew him decades ago, and he had worked all over the world with many hundreds of other dancers since then. He would never know how deeply he had affected me, and who knows how many of those others?

I unlocked my bike slowly, and cycled home through Berkeley traffic to my family who would by now all be home waiting for me, and the chicken roasting in the oven would be ready for its last-minute garnish of crushed lemon peel and garlic.

Donald McKayle is gone now. So is John.

I could be next...

But the living still must eat...

The Healing of Humiliation

Who doesn't have stories? I certainly do. Growing up in wartime in a family of frightened Jews, I took in their fear and anger with every breath. My child's body was acquainted with grief, and I learned to swallow down tears until I could no longer feel the sorrow, and years of clamping down on my gut created an unattractive belly bloat that no amount of dieting has ever been able to reduce.

As sorrow determined my shape, so it determined my life, since all I ever wanted to do was dance, to twirl and leap on a stage wild and free! But those were the days of Balanchine's stick-thin ballet dancers, and a girl with hips and a belly wasn't even encouraged to take lessons, much less aspire to be a dancer. Even so, that was what *this* girl felt she was born for.

I danced in my dreams—still do—and choreographed every daytime step I took, climbing stairs, walking down the street, bending over to pet a dog. This embarrassed my mother no end so when she caught me at it she would hiss between tight teeth, "Stop making a fool of yourself!"

So my sense of self worth was questionable from early on, and I'm still trying to heal that. The process is arduous, but worth it, I think, even at my age. I am at last learning to admire the plucky kid I was then and what my particular gifts are good for. Anything less than self-acceptance, it seems to me now, is a huge waste of time.

Gradually, I bring breath into my lower belly where that toxic dump of hard-packed shame lies. Breathing in from as deep down as my breath can go, I dislodge old emotions of self-hate and humiliation, examining them carefully and letting the tears come. How many uncountable years have I allowed that poison to reside in my blood? And why?

My lower spine has more room now and I let it flex and twist into longed-for movement as my dancer-soul spirals back into my limbs. Breathe. Hiding and habitual shame fade as I begin to shift into the comfort zone of my birthright.

This amazing healing process fascinates me! I feel like a detective tracking down subtle clues from bloodstains on the floor of my life. They lead me into old closed rooms of my body where assumptions of not being good enough morph into feelings of being better than everyone else! I am shocked by what I find hiding there— old mean-spirited envy lurking in corners all squished up against self-righteous judgment—the shadow sides of all my deep humiliations projected outwards!

How embarrassing! But I recognize how those feelings of self-doubt can lead to fundamentalism, Right or Left, along with the arsenal of guns in bedrooms for protection against perceived enemies. We who mistrust ourselves deep down cannot help but project it onto other people, not realizing that the 'enemy' actually resides deep within ourselves where we are too ashamed to look.

So our pain becomes blame, and then we vote those into power who fan the flame of our fears. As a society, we've gotten way too good at that. Perhaps to find our way out of this conundrum we might start digging deep into our own fears and see what may be lurking there. And then try and clean it up.

Nobody ever said it would be easy. We humans are well meaning as a species, but quite imperfect—we really can be a clumsy bunch!

Many years ago, during a trip to New York to see my publisher, I decided to hire a taxicab for a day to visit scenes of my childhood, especially places where I had experienced a child's pain and humiliation: old neighborhoods, my grade school, the beach at Coney Island, and finally the Home for Incurables where my Grandma had sat out her life, paralyzed by multiple sclerosis, in a wooden wheelchair.

My driver, Kenny and I became intimate friends that day. He waited patiently at each of our stops, discreetly turning away when I stood on the sidewalks and cried. At every stop I found exactly the spot where I had once been shamed, and there felt again the pain of that long ago time. When it had faded, I took in deep breaths and blew them out, letting the negative energy dissipate into the ordinary air of the present moment. Like that, I went around New York City clearing one place after another of the sorrows of my personal past.

At P.S. 215 I stood outside my first grade classroom where I had once been sent in punishment for 'losing' a paper my father had actually refused to sign—I covered for him, saying I had lost it; in the schoolyard I found the place I had fallen on my face and broken my two front teeth. At my old house on Billings Place in Brooklyn I stood right on the spot my mother had once pounded me with her fists for rolling in the snow with a boy.

Kenny and I drove around until we found the restaurant in which, on my wedding day and in front of the guests, my father had slapped my face for disobeying him. It took a while to neutralize that one. Then we hiked down the hill under the Whitestone Bridge where Herb had proposed to me, and we sat there quietly for awhile by the water.

Kenny listened to each story as we made our way through the Boroughs, nodding his head in sympathy and asking leading questions. In the Bronx around the corner of the Beth Abraham Home for Jewish Incurables where I knew in my cells every sight and sound and smell of the wasted souls inside, we stopped for lunch first at Weinstein's Delicatessen, as the family had done in the past before going in to see my Grandmother. It was fortification then, and it was fortification now.

I ordered my old comfort food, a sliced tongue sandwich on rye with root beer soda, and a pickle. Kenny had a pastrami sandwich, I recall, and we shared two root beers while I told him, with shaking breath, about going to see my Grandma in this hospital every Sunday of my life, choking on the stench of human misery week after week until I learned to take it like a grown-up!

"Do you want me to come in with you?" he asked quietly.

"I think I've got to do this alone, Kenny," I replied.

When I later emerged from the hospital, ragged and sad, Kenny took me to Howard's Beach where he had played as a boy, and told me *his* stories, driving me to some of the scenes of his childhood and reminiscing about growing up Black in the Bronx.

It was a day of redemption for both of us, two people who had not met before this day and would likely never meet again.

Thank you, Kenny, and God bless you.

I find myself taking a similar trip now, as I enter this next phase of my life, going through letters and memories, making amends and seeking forgiveness, bowing to shades of people no longer here, apologizing and explaining, laughing and crying. I hope to leave as few negative traces as possible.

To all of you, living and dead, whose lives have touched mine, please forgive me if I have hurt you; I did not mean to do so. I also forgive those of you who have hurt me, whether you meant to or not.

I had a dream the other night that I was in the rehearsal studio of my favorite dance company, the LINES Ballet, hanging out with the dancers before a rehearsal. We were all improvising—just fooling

113

around and laughing a lot—and when Alonzo King, the choreographer, came in to start the warm-up, I moved to the side of the space to watch.

"Where're you going?" he asked.

"To watch," I replied.

"Why?"

Embarrassed, I muttered the obvious. "I'm not thin, I'm old and I'm not in the company."

"Says who?" he replied. "Of course you're in the company! Get back out there!"

So I did.

Whatever was I thinking? Of course I am in the company!

As we all are, warts and bulges and all.

Hurting

for Carol M.

Sitting around the campfire on my brother's farm with friends late one night last summer, I stood up to shake out a stiff knee when I lost my balance and stumbled backwards, falling and catching my hand in the metal spring of a folding chair that snapped shut like a vise onto my knuckles.

It was the very definition of a 'freak accident.'

Picture it: a woman of a certain age splayed flat on the grass on a moonless night helplessly clamped to a metal chair, the Milky Way frothy in the sky above and a dozen people surrounding her in shock, not knowing what in the world had just happened.

Nor did I. I knew only excruciating pain, the way a bear caught in a steel trap must feel. I had all but stopped breathing. Then, coming from I know not where, I heard in my head clear instructions about what to do next:

"Use it! Use your pain!" was what I heard. "Look for your calm core on the other side of the pain. Breathe, focus on the hurt and notice your emotions—fear, denial, embarrassment." It told me to welcome any help offered, and to maintain a sense of humor at my predicament—my hand caught in a *chair?*

"You are showing the others, especially the young ones, how to respond to pain when the going gets rough."

At that, my horrible pain then morphed into *interesting* pain—and I found I could indeed handle it. My buddies around the campfire went right into action. I got to observe my daughter as the remarkable healer she is and felt the power of a community coming together to support one of their own. My niece, I recall, had the job of distracting me by telling a funny story about when her dog got lost, keeping us all in stitches, and my job was to look at her and not my hand, and to keep breathing as calmly as I could.

Once the ambulance crew arrived from town, it took three strong guys with crowbars to unhitch the spring that clamped me down to that damned chair! My hand looked awful, the back skin having been scraped off down to tendon and bone, but I'd been caught across the knuckles where the hand is fleshy, so no fingers were broken, no tendons snapped. I was lucky, and to everyone's amazement, still calm even though it hurt like hell!

Later, sewn up in the Emergency Room of the hospital in town and sent back to the farm bruised but not broken, I realized that I had not, for one moment, been left alone with my pain. My daughter never left my side. The others came in relays, sat with us, supplied us with snacks and told us how fabulous we were!

We were. And could be again, I now know. We can make it through these hard times by staying calm, breathing and doing what needs to be done—always with help from our friends.

The most painful part happened at the airport a few days later.

"Unwrap the bandage," I was told curtly by the young female security agent.

"What?"

My hand had been skillfully wrapped to protect it from the inevitable bumps and stresses it would receive getting on and off an airplane. There was no way I could neatly unwrap those layers of gauze and cotton and get them back on again with one hand. I assumed she was joking, but she meant it; I had to take the bloody thing off so this young woman could personally see my bruises and stitched flesh and be sure I was not hiding a weapon!

"Eeuw gross!" she exclaimed at the sight, letting me through to trail bloody gauze behind me and look for a quiet corner in the Concourse to re-wrap my hand, where I cried—for her more than for myself—and for our culture that, in the name of 'security' demands heartlessness from our own young people.

At last, my accident had brought me to tears.

Now, less than a year later, it is only in my heart you might find evidence of a scar.

We are all carrying scars, deep ones: for the children languishing in detention centers at the "border;" for our fellow citizens so scared they would vote a madman into high office; for the forests still being destroyed for profit and for the icecaps melting into polluted oceans; for the droughts and the floods, the hungry and the homeless of every race, the children, the frightened children.

We are scarred—and scared—every last one of us whether we realize it or not.

I am watching how my good friend Carol is handling her own wounds now, after she and her husband lost their home in one of the big fires in Northern California. They got out with their lives, but little else.

They had barely caught their breaths after the fire when one of their adult children lost his job, followed by a grandchild getting racked up in a car accident! Her shock level went way over the top and her therapist alerted the authorities, fearful she might kill herself!

Carol, who is neither a large nor self-destructive woman, was dragged off to the local Psychiatric ward, she told me later, by six policemen, two firemen, two security guards and two ambulance drivers, who threatened to tie her down if she didn't stop fighting them! When she told me the story later, we laughed until we were weak. The fact is that she is one of the sanest, most grounded women I know.

SIX policemen??

So, when we stop shaking our heads in wonder, we've been asking ourselves: What do you do when so much has been taken away that you are left with almost nothing except life itself?

Her response, in her feisty way is, "If life has given me scraps, well then I suppose I'm just going to have to make a quilt!"

Me too! So we're going to do it together. Fortunately, we both love old fabrics—people like us have been called 'quilting maniacs'—so we're comfortable with unsorted piles of scraps.

Her scraps may be gone, but I've got enough for both of us on shelves and in boxes, collected over decades. Anyhow, she loves haunting thrift stores, finding old embroidery on worn-out pillowcases, velvet ribbons, silk sashes, old batiks.

One day soon we'll get together, kneel on my living room floor and lay out our stashes by color. As we place golds next to purples and decide if we want patchwork or log cabin squares, I'll ask about the family, and she'll tell me about the latest 'catastrophe.'

She will laugh … I probably will not, but I will listen, quietly placing pink satin next to a vivid black-and-white check while she talks.

Inevitably, we'll get to our marriages and then politics, probably crying together about the two children who have already died in detention at the border. Sorting through scraps of calico and bits of raw silk, we'll take bets on the country waking up quickly enough to make a difference before Plump finally self-destructs, and then lay out a log cabin square with a centerpiece of cherry-red satin.

I'll go to the sewing machine to sew it up while she cuts and irons pieces for the next square.

We'll no doubt wonder together about next year's fire season, about whether the Democrats will listen to all the smart young women of color taking the places of the old-guard guys, about how to start changing the money system that's got it all backwards.

"I love how this red satin looks in the center," one of us will say.

"What about this off-white lace for the border?" the other will offer. When the square is sewn up and ironed out flat, we will sit back, admiring the new square in quiet for awhile. Then we'll embrace in a deep long hug.

"Ready for some tea?" I'll suggest.

"Sure," she'll murmur, sighing from deep down.

Then I'll get up and put the kettle on, waiting and musing while the water comes to a boil.

Up in the Air

for Adriel Heisey

Several years ago I had the great good fortune to fly above the Sonoran Desert in Arizona with a wonderful aerial photographer in his hand-built ultra-light plane, in search of prehistoric ruins. We took off from Tucson in pre-dawn darkness, the wind in our faces and our feet dangling in plain air—and my heart in my mouth—and we communicated through walkie-talkies in our helmets.

We leveled at 600 feet just as the sun came over the horizon, and looked down searching for evidence of ancient human life in this deceptively monotonous landscape. Flying low enough to make out details on the ground, we were also high enough to get a wide perspective of the lay of land beneath us.

"I live for this!" Adriel crowed, as we searched for our ancient layered past in the desert landscape below. "I fly for wonder!"

With him I was flying for wonder too, learning from him about the land and time, about different perspectives, about the borders between places and between one human being and another.

We played with borders in the air, flying back and forth over the imaginary line between Mexico and the US, seeing only continuous desert. "There's no real border with Mexico," he told me. "This was all indigenous land until the 16th century when the Spanish came in and made that part *theirs*. That's like a few seconds ago in earthtime!"

We found sites wherever we looked: ancient terraces and stone enclosures, dancing grounds and what looked like a racetrack! We flew over enormous drawings etched into the desert pan and ritual gathering places tucked deep into canyons. We even found evidence of dinosaurs! Adriel recorded the positions of each site we found and filmed them in their surround. Some were new to him, and some already familiar to the archaeologists.

My role was as sharp-eyed lookout.

On our third trip out, a year later, we flew over Picacho Peak, breasting clouds above the summit and emerging into sunlit spaces only to plunge back into obscuring whiteness where neither we nor the mountain seemed to have any anchors in reality. Descending from clouds to circle our way down the mountain again, we came close enough to all but touch the crumbly yellow sandstone and smell the pitted rock.

Same mountain—different perspective.

Landing below at the tiny airport, we grabbed our packs and found the trail, hiking up in the hot sun and bending to smell flowering agaves, following the flights of birds and the scurrying of beetles, hearing dry rock crackle beneath our feet.

Same mountain—entirely new perspective.

At one switchback in the trail, I felt so happy that I called out to Adriel, "I'm so glad you're in the world at the same time I am!" and we exchanged a smile I will never forget.

Sigh—yet another perspective of Picacho Peak.

That was some twenty years ago, but I am thinking of it now, wondering about perspective and how to understand what we have to face now, as we and the world are going through a major shift of consciousness, and we have lost our bearings. Frightened by the enormity of the challenge, we have no idea of the scale of the mountain we are trying to climb.

So what do we do now and how can we understand what is happening?

Is this about politics, about religion, about climate change or all of the above and more? What does it mean to 'shift', anyhow? Who knows? I just know that whatever it is we are supposed to do now, it is *big* and it will take great strength and courage.

I know that whenever I've had to stand up to personal disasters I had no control over—not infrequent, I'm afraid—it took every bit if my will to face it straight on, even when I thought I could not survive such humiliation.

Until I was about fourteen I simply cocooned into my own thoughts and went blank when the family dramas were beyond my endurance. But when my need to dance began to make me crazy, and dance classes were vetoed yet again, I did what was, until that moment, impossible: I went to audition with the director of Deerwood Music and Dance Camp, offering to work in the kitchen for free in exchange for classes with Donald McKayle at Deerwood. The Director looked puzzled, but asked me kindly,

"Why don't you just come as a student?"

"My parents wouldn't let me," I mumbled, shamed down to my roots. His nostrils flared white, I recall—I loved him for that—and he offered to come to my house that Sunday and talk to them. I could hardly believe he would do that.

"I'll be there at 11 in the morning," he told me. Make sure they're at home, but don't tell them I'm coming. Of course you do not need to work in the kitchen to dance!" he added.

He did indeed show up that Sunday, observed that it was not a matter of money, skillfully shamed my parents into supporting my wish to dance, and stood tall and rather fierce while my father made out a check for my tuition at Deerwood.

The rest is history and I bless Sherwood Kains forever.

Perspective and guts, that's what we need now, as the world we live in ricochets wildly all over the place like a balloon with the air let out.

I wonder if this period of dissolution we are in is writ into a much larger Plan that rises and falls in cycles, each turn of the wheel bringing our souls into a higher frequency of vibration as we experience new lessons of embodiment in physical bodies? Is it possible that this period is about the old structures breaking down—and not a moment too soon—so that we can start fresh with a more expanded vision and build it all up again in new ways, based upon an improved, more sane, more loving model?

We are certainly more than ready for it! Perhaps it is no accident that people like our President are here to help take the old structures apart, setting the stage for our young ones to step in with their visions and energy to create a whole new way of living upon this beautiful and damaged planet.

I choose to think of him as a scapegoat and consummate actor, bless his heart. But we're up the task, aren't we?

Aren't we?

We have just enough time to catch the planet's environment before it all melts and goes down the drain, and so many ways to do so. We won't likely get our old world back, but that's not the point as there's a bigger perspective for us to see—the Whole mountain and not just the individual rocks.

Creation happens at every moment, they say, and I've experienced it more than once in my life—the surprise, the beauty, the unexpected visions. I've flown in the sky while the setting sun sank red beneath a slightly curved horizon, the lands and waters below deepening into mysterious shadow. I've felt it in the presence of a beloved friend who made me glad to be alive in that very moment.

The stones that form a mountain are as essential to the mountain as the handclasp of friendship on the trail is essential to the world.

In the Science of Physics, every period of disequilibrium leads to reorganization into a finer, more complex system of organization. This is built into the world! I also believe—get this—that everyone here now has chosen to be here to take on this task.

It is time; it's more than time. As Sherwood Kains knew to come at the eleventh hour—literally—it is time for us all to show up too, each in our own way.

Because it's not too late—yet.

Polyamory,
Aging & the Bulls

There is, where I live, a young couple who take part in a community of 'polyamorists,' which means that each of them has multiple lovers, and everyone involved considers the others—and their children—a kind of extended family. They celebrate birthdays together, exchange childcare and all take the occasional trip together.

It's rather cosy.

Since my particular neighbors work different hours and each have more than one extra partner, the designated 'Love Room'—(my designation, as it is within close audible distance from my 'Studio Room')—gets quite a bit of use in the course of an average week. Noisy use.

As I work at home writing and teaching in my studio, it inevitably means I cannot help but hear the variety of activities that go on there at all hours of the day—and night. One time, an amorous session even got recorded as I was giving an interview outside in the garden!

On principle I rather like the easy-going free-spiritedness of these young folks experimenting with family and sexual relationships. It's time we brought fresh air into the bogged-down nuclear family scene that doesn't work so well for most people, really, with bored couples, single parents and confused children, everyone longing for love. I see these poly folks' kids doing fine with the arrangement and the adults all have that rosy glow of healthy sex.

But the ongoing distractions of passionate encounters within earshot while I work, while I have lunch, while I meet with people is, frankly, getting old. Despite myself I notice I've begun listening with a novelist's, or maybe even a Peeping Tom's, ear to their goings-on. I work out the perfect phrases to describe this or that phase of foreplay; I note the variations of timing; I wonder who that guy is who seems to be having a hard time …

Despite myself, since the activities are impossible to tune out, I am using them as material. I *am* a writer, after all. Or maybe just a dirty old lady …

But the other night I really knew I was in trouble when I was awakened in the wee hours before dawn by the deep moaning of what sounded like the biggest orgasm of all time, and I sat up in bed startled and furious! This was over-the-top, insensitive, anti-social behavior, intrusive, totally distracting and it was starting to drive me crazy! Enough already! I would go read these people the riot act and tell them to take their insatiable lovemaking elsewhere!

Except, realizing that my husband wasn't lying in bed next to me, I wasn't at home. I was asleep in a room 100 miles from where I live, on retreat in the country. As I woke up further and the moaning continued I was totally confused until I recognized the lowing of bulls in the pasture expressing themselves as bulls do: rhythmic moans rising into shrieks, again and again. Maybe they were lovesick, maybe just plain greeting the dawn or each other in a bullsy way. Big black bulls!

I leaned over and laughed myself silly until the laughter turned into tears, and I cried for the sexy woman I had once been—in my prime…

… when I was young …

Are Crop Circles Real?

Herb and I had a loving and good marriage all our adult lives, but one subject had the power to drive us apart, and that was 'Crop Circles.' His scientific mind simply would not entertain the possibility of an unknown 'something' creating huge, spectacular artworks in farmers' wheat fields. My own intuitive way of thinking, of course, welcomed them.

In any case, these gorgeous designs—by the *hundreds, and later by the thousands*—were not just products of my imagination; they were right there on the ground to be witnessed firsthand, and walked through and photographed by anybody who came by!

"They must be done by a bunch of really clever art students!" Herb insisted.

"All over the world?" I argued, "and in plants that are bent but not broken? And nobody either claiming them or charging money for them?"

Which, in itself would be something of a miracle!

We actually had a yelling match the summer of 1990 when I returned from a walking trip in England where I'd entered, and photographed the first pictogram to appear in a wheat field in Wiltshire—a sensational formation of circles and lines stretching the length of two football fields. The farmers who let us into their fields were as baffled as the rest of us.

"It wasn't here when we left last night," they told us, "but this morning we found this! Not even a footprint left behind, nothing. The dogs didn't even bark in the night!"

We all got shivers.

The word was already getting out and curiosity seekers like myself had begun arriving at this remote farm in the Wiltshire wheat fields by early the next morning. As it happened, I was already in the area, visiting Mary Scott who lived two villages over, a healer and author whose books on earth energies I had admired for years. In the bus station coming there, I had noticed an article about the strange formation on that day's news board, and my timing and destination, as it turned out, were impeccable.

Perfect magic!

At the farm in Alton Barnes I became part of the most unusual party I had ever attended, with dowsers and healers and thrill seekers and tourists all tromping into the wheat with their cameras ready, and military helicopters buzzing overhead like noisy mosquitos.

I slowly walked alone down the length of the formation to the far end, kneeling to examine a delicate rick-rack design at the edge of the lay. The sun was hot, the air straw-fragrant and examining it up close I counted exactly nine individual stalks lying between each separate point of the design! And I started to cry.

Now, almost thirty years, and thousands of these spectacular artworks—worldwide—later, we still do not know how and why they were created. Nor by whom.

Some of us who are interested in sacred geometry, though, can make guesses because their geometries match ancient sacred geometry, profound with messages about the nature of a reality far beyond our three-dimensional understandings of the world. These geometric designs seem to be speaking in code, about important changes we would do well to pay attention to.

Many indigenous cultures speak of signs appearing at the endings of earth ages, which many claim is Now. Perhaps these colossal works of art are indeed gentle signs to prepare us for major changes in the offing, rather than waiting for catastrophes giving the same message! I wonder why we persist in denying beautiful miracles right there in plain sight just because we do not yet have the science to explain them? What are we so scared of?

As it is, the debunkers have been busy stirring up their campaigns to deny the importance of these happenings, the hoaxers have been hired to try and mimic the genuine circles, and sadly, many of the original group of researchers have died.

Others, like myself, have backed away from the mean-spirited controversies out there, but despite all that, the formations in the fields continue to appear across the world, all the same.

I just saw an aerial photograph of two magnificent new circles, spun in trees, rather than wheat, in a forest in Japan!

Imagine …

Mary and I spent a week together, talking non-stop on all the subjects that impassioned both of us and wondering what was happening in those fields so close to her village?

"And how did you manage to arrive here all the way from America just when this is happening right here in this lazy corner of the world?" she asked me archly. Actually, I had no idea.

Neither did she, but we were both clearly affected by some unusual energies because one night after leaving her cottage for the True Heart pub a mile away where I was staying, she told me to go right to bed after having something to eat. We had gone deep that day; but when I arrived at the pub, the local farmers were waiting to teach me how to play darts with them!

So of course, I did. And shocked everyone, including myself, by hitting a perfect Bull's Eye—precisely in the center of the central ring—on my first throw!

It was pandemonium in there! This American lady … and she throws a dart … her first dart! …. And she hits the bulls-eye! They regaled me with cheers and beers, and considered carrying me on their shoulders but I wouldn't let them—and then the kitchen phone rang—for me! It was Mary calling me from her house a mile down the road.

"I told you to stay quiet," she said without preamble. "We did a lot of work today, and you need stillness."

"But how did you know …?" I spluttered. There was no way she could have heard the pandemonium in the pub from her cottage a mile away. "I just hit a bull's eye, Mary!"

Quietly, she replied, "Well bully for you, but you won't hit another, so go to bed!"

I will never understand how she knew, nor if the energies emanating from the crop circle in Alton Barnes had anything to do with my perfect aim and her perfect knowing.

Changes are happening, as the indigenous ones have been telling us, and it would do us well to pay close attention to signs and portents, especially those happening to ourselves.

I imagine Herb is quite aware now of the multiple dimensions the crop circles are pointing to. He might say, from his new perspective,

"The world is much more immense, and so much more dimensioned than you can imagine! More is possible than you can dream of! Pictures in wheat may be the easy part …"

In fact, he did report back to me as he was dying, while he was still able to, telling me what he was seeing—a universe of "worlds and worlds and worlds" spiraling out there just beyond our ordinary human vision. With his hand he made spirals in the air and gazed at me through luminous eyes bright with awe.

He died peacefully that night. Yes.

The rest is mostly silence.

Getting through Hard Times

Many years ago, on the day before I was to perform with a local dance company, a fellow Zen student was shot and killed near the Meditation Center, and I completely fell apart. There was no way I felt I could get through a performance, especially as the evening started with my solo—my first big chance to show myself as a dancer.

I was in quivering shock.

Herb got me dressed and to the venue in time for company warm-up, where I stumbled through the motions in a daze. When the curtain opened for my solo, I found myself onstage and blinded by the stage lights, but as I began to dance my body took over, and I improvised a dance of grief rather than the choreography I had rehearsed.

It was only when the music changed and the Company joined me onstage for the remainder of the piece, that I came out of my daze and realized what I had done. I was mortified, and fled the stage after we'd taken our bows, sobbing in Herb's arms and dreading that I still had to come back the next night for another performance!

But when I arrived the next evening full of apologies, wonder of wonders, the other dancers grabbed me in bear hugs. "Where did you disappear to last night?" they demanded. "Everyone came backstage looking for you! You made the piece! Do it again!"

So now I keep being reminded about the power of art to heal, especially when the artists are fine at their crafts and able to use them to transmit deep emotion that resonates with our shared human experience.

I know a violist—my daughter, in fact—who understands the power of her art to heal, and plays in homeless shelters, prisons and hospitals. I watch how the visionary choreographer Alonzo King uses dance as his medium, speaking the universal language of the body in motion to transmit our deepest emotions. And since they've hit the stage, I've watched two young Croatian cellists play from a depth of soul rare in such young people, and make it clear that their intent is to bring us together through the universal language of music.

These amazing young men were no doubt inspired as children by the "cellist of Sarajevo," the man who took to the streets with his cello during the infamous Siege of Sarajevo. After witnessing the murder of twenty-two of his neighbors as they stood on line at the bakery shop near his apartment, this cellist went out into the concrete rubble with his cello, reassuring himself and his neighbors that beauty and generosity still existed in the world.

Each day he went out to play in the bombed-out streets of his neighborhood. I do not know if snipers eventually got him—I think not—but his spirit has survived into the next generation with these two amazing young cellists who play like angels and are letting us know that the world can indeed be beautiful despite everything, as the cellist of Sarajevo was saying during a horrific war that lasted four years.

Now, though, this next generation of musicians can perform on the world stage, as modern technology brings them right into our lives on screens that fit into our pockets, reassuring us that hope and joy can be found everywhere, even in a land torn by war a mere generation ago.

Stjepan Hauser and Luka Šulić—look them up!

Beauty, art and love in the face of a world going crazy may be just what we need now, in all the ways we can provide it for one another. I bless these young cellists their vision, their extraordinary talent and their wide open hearts. Whenever I feel discouraged, I listen to them.

As Stjepan put it in an interview,

"We want to get people out of their seats, from seven years to seventy years, so happy they all jump and sing together!"

I can feel in my bones what moves these young musicians, and what moved the cellist of Sarajevo, and if I had been there during the war I hope I would also have had the guts to go down into the streets between bombings to dance in the rubble. If I were a singer, I hope I would have had the courage to climb the bell tower and sing my heart out there. If I were a painter, I'd have liked to have painted on the bombed-out walls with *anything* I found there—lipstick, charred wood, clods of earth!

As it is, I am a writer, and so I write.

And you?

Apologizing to God

for the women of Sweet Honey in the Rock

In the sweet light of morning the other day, I stood in the garden in bare feet savoring the tart juice of a plum just fallen from the tree. The birds were busily flitting through the branches and knocking ripe plums to the ground, chattering like all get out.

Suddenly my internal vision shifted and these birds and this plum tree took place in untold eons of Time and Space where generations of birds and trees had evolved from the inborn urge to procreate and feed. I saw, in that moment, the germs of life emerging from sparks of desire to make a world, taking form through deep oceans and emerging from comets and explosions of fire and the spinning of a planet preparing for the experiment of Life.

I could feel God's longing to create something new, and It Was Good.

The vision shifted back to the here and now as I swallowed the plum skin, the birds still bickering above me. For a moment I held the Big Picture side by side with that ordinary moment, feeling myself in both simultaneously—my tongue tasting the sweetness of plum juice, while my inner eyes watched galaxies forming in Space.

But then a few days later I awoke from a nightmare of wicked guys in my kitchen stealing food I had just cooked for my children, stuffing it into their own mouths. I fought them desperately, kicking and yelling as they beat me away from their food-filled hands. My own screaming woke me up. I was still thrashing as the nightmare faded, and all day long I had a stomach ache, my guts continuing to fight for my children's supper—my children and all the hungry children in detention cells at the border, who are our children.

Yes, mine! And yours!

Forgive us, God, for we know not what we do.

Now, I must confess I do not believe in 'a God' *per se,* but rather in the Consciousness that is 'Love' in the Universe. To me, this is the frequency that is our birthright, because it is where we have come from and what we are made of.

To me, there is nothing, nor was there ever anything in existence that is not God.

Hard to put into words—it's more an intuitive knowing, a certainty on the skin that everything in the Universe is conscious and interconnected. My ways of understanding this are the subtle wake-ups of feeling that happen when I fall in love, or hear music or am dancing, my heart rising with gratitude for this gift of life in a world that seems to have tried out everything.

I mean, whoever could dream up flamingos, or redwood trees, or even us humans, for that matter? It's got to be some creative force with a sense of humor, don't you think?

Fine with me if you want to call it God.

I went to a concert by Sweet Honey In The Rock the other night, and got a good reminder of that all-encompassing Spirit through these powerful and gifted women who sing like angels and tell it like it is! This ensemble of Black singers have been lifting my spirit for years with their music, getting down and getting angry, pouring out their passion and you better be ready to respond with your own! It is music and prayer and being real and beautiful in the face of the mixed-up glory and insanity that is our world.

They are not ashamed to be strong and they do not mince words. They preach at full voice, loud and clear and what they preach is LOVE!

Let us say *Amen*.

How dare any bad guys come to steal the food we've prepared for our children—your children or mine?

NOOOOO! Y'all hear now??

I came home reassured that no matter what happens, we're here making waves and music to beat the band, and won't stop even when Judgment Day lets us know we're gonna have to change, whoever we are, no matter how rich or what neighborhood we live in.

Nobody ever said it would be easy and anyhow, if it were too easy we'd probably be too lazy to pay attention.

As the Croatian cellist Stjepan Hauser who performs everything from Bach to Hard Rock in huge arenas said in a recent interview,

> *The world needs every kind of music played with a big heart because it can make you a better human being. We want this music to go mainstream, for little kids and Grandpas and people of all ages—everywhere in the world. If it does, there will be peace—I promise.*

That, of course, is the hope.

Meanwhile, I've been reading about recurring cataclysms on the planet—yup, I read that sort of thing—and it seems our civilization is neither the first nor the last nor the only one to have inhabited this Earth. Periodically, disaster ensues and erases most of the evidence of anyone being there before: floods, fires, asteroids, earthquakes. But they were here, it turns out.

Untold ages of highly developed cultures have existed here long before us, and Freddy Silva, who researches the evidences of these civilizations, concludes that humankind is way older than any of us realize, and has been far more advanced in the past than we are today. He says in his recent book, *The Missing Lands,*

> *… it is reassuring to know that the only constants in the universe are order and chaos, the higher the level of chaos, the greater the potential to jump to a higher level of order.*

I take comfort in that. If it's all a big mess right now, it's not a total disaster but rather an awkward transition towards a higher level of order. We're in crouch position, ready to spring forward, and while the temptation to sink into the ground and take a nap may be great, I wouldn't suggest we do so.

It's time to take a deep breath, accept that we're all in this together, hold hands tight and get ready to jump!

And be ingenious, and laugh a lot, and dance and swing your hips and fall in love with somebody, and cook up supper for one another and sing! Like Sweet Honey in the Rock, and sing it loud! Keep your eyes on the prize, hold on! hold on!

Hold on … hold on … hold on!

Psychic Disclosure

I had an interview with a reporter a few days ago from the Los Angeles Times, about my current work with affordable housing. We had a good talk over tea and a snack of dried apricots and cashews. The journalist stared at the bowl when I offered it to him, and then blurted out, "What made you put out cashews and apricots? We've never met before, have we?"

I had no idea what he was talking about until he explained that he has a kind of fetish for cashews and dried apricots—in fact, a bag of it was tucked in his backpack at that moment right across the room,— and most people don't put those two things together!

I laughed, because this kind of coincidence happens to me all the time. I believe it's a kind of inborn ability we all have, but since it isn't encouraged in our culture, we rarely even notice when it happens.

I wonder if those of us whose childhoods were difficult, tend to develop our intuitive radars early on to help us through the emotional minefields of our early years? In any case, it is fairly commonplace for me to do this sort of thing unawares: like serving a stranger his favorite, but unusual snack.

My days are filled with stories like this, some having serious consequences—but that's a conversation for another day. The truth is that not everybody loves me for my unbidden ability that can come over as threatening or too weird for some people. Mostly, though, I get away with it and good things happen.

"How did you do that?" my scientist husband asked me again and again over the years when I pulled off timely coincidences that he considered impossible. I have truthfully never had an answer.

Over the years I've learned to trust my intuition implicitly, although I've chosen to keep quiet about it so as not to be thought of as a witch. I do not enjoy scaring people.

"Reality is more vast, more dimensioned and more loving than we have been taught," reports Eben Alexander, a neurosurgeon who survived a near-death experience and saw the "many-faceted, many-dimensioned, interconnected, conscious universe." He goes on to say that we belong to it all, not just to the material layer which, though beautiful and remarkable, would not exist without the infinite and vastly more wondrous Whole from which it comes, and that we all have access to that Whole even when we do not realize it.

For me, it is the largest context of existence, interconnected and interdependent, that I believe in. Just as a tree belongs to its context of earth and roots, soil and fungal web beneath it, and is dependent upon the air and sun and rain for its life, so are we part of an interconnected web of life—a whole universe that is part and parcel of who we are.

Our culture's materialist mindset tends to call this way of thinking 'woo-woo.' I honestly have no idea why.

But we've come to a crisis of belief, and if we stay stuck in our too-tight paradigm of materialism, we are all in danger of self-destructing, I believe. The clues that it is time to let go of habitual ways of thinking appear before us on a daily basis, and we collectively walk blindly past them, too scared to let go and melt into the reality of the larger context of our lives.

However, woo-woo or not, I live by it every day, even when I am considered dangerous to those who fear what they do not understand. But it's time for me to come out of the closet because we're in vast trouble now as we go through the eye of this needle. Our consciousness has *got* to expand if we are to survive!

This is *serious*, folks!

We are being shown a way through, year after year by patient unseen artists who present their artworks on the grand scale all over the world. We have yet to be collectively willing to pay attention—probably because we have to change our minds about a lot of things in order to accept that this phenomenon—called 'Crop Circles'—may not be a crazy hoax, but may be Real!

Eeeks!

Since they are hidden in plain sight, all over the planet, it may require a relaxed suspension of disbelief on our parts. We may have to just look at it without trying to figure it out because these artworks keep appearing and can be visited right there on the ground. People photograph them, walk in them, argue about them, work out the complex geometries represented in the designs, but the media ignores them as if they did not exist.

Or worse, calls them "just hoaxes!"

How silly when just a bit of awareness and a small shift of perception could help humanity evolve just by being open to the possibility that these massive artworks may be a creative demonstration that the universe, and thus ourselves, are even bigger and more complex than we thought!

This is not so much about designs appearing mysteriously in fields and forests all over the world—it is about Us, I believe. We have a chance to open our imaginations to a larger and deeper reality than we thought was there! How wonderful is that?

Especially if it might help us and our planet through this excruciating time in the world.

I came upon my first Crop Circle in England by a series of synchronicities that required finding myself, unawares, exactly at the right place at the right time. I had staggered off the Cornwall Coast Trail after walking one hundred miles with a friend and was next off to visit the writer Mary Scott in Wiltshire.

I had to find my way by foot to a specific bus stop in a small coastal town to catch the bus going my way. But for the magic to work, I had to coincide with the drop-off of that morning's newspaper to see its front-page photograph of a massive design in wheat that had just appeared in a farmer's field in the Vale of Pewsey where, as it happened, was near where my friend lived! The rest is history.

Simple as pie—or cashews and apricots.

I wonder a lot, as a writer, about how to describe what mystical consciousness feels like in my body. To me, it simply comes naturally, so I don't know what all the hullabaloo is about. I just know it is about 'feeling' rather than 'thinking.'

I suspect we all have moments when the "ceiling opens up and we see the sky" as my friend Ann has put it. Who has not felt the ecstasy of falling madly in love; swooned to music that makes you ache; stood in the first rain after a long drought; had an orgasm that shook you half blind with pleasure?

For a moment we touch the ineffable and experience awe.

All that and more is what I'm talking about. It is about knowing in our whole beings the deep joy of the Mystery that underlies all phenomena of our physical world, the Mystery that is love itself. It is an energy, a vibration, a consciousness, a gratitude, a feeling that we all have access to.

Once we recognize the high frequency 'feel' of this joy, we can find our way back to it easily when those who are frightened by us try to shame us into silence.

All we need is fifty-one percent of the people accessing the higher vibrations of authentic joy to save us all from going over the brink.

Just think, only fifty-one percent of us who know how to love, can save the world!

Sanctuary Я Us

for Bayo Akomolafe and baby Rylan

Yesterday morning a photographer appeared unexpectedly at the door to take photographs for an article that would be appearing in a small local newspaper. I had no idea this would be happening, had not yet washed my face and was wearing different-colored socks.

"They told me you were teaching this morning, and to get shots of you dancing," he told me.

He was a stocky fellow with a bright smile and a camera slung across his chest. I asked him to wait while I combed my hair.

Meanwhile, Fascist clouds are gathering across the world and children are locked up in cells; fires are raging in the Arctic and guns are bought legally by malcontents … and I was taking the stairs two at a time to grab a hairbrush and change my socks … to pose, dancing, for a man with a strong accent who had appeared at my door.

Stranger things have happened …

In the studio he followed the action, clicking away, and when I suggested he put down the camera and join us, he did! We spent all the rest of his time there dancing wildly together, and he went away happy.

I live for these unexpected adventures the universe provides! This was all happening because an article has just been written about my donation of our longtime family home to a non-profit organization for affordable housing.

After over 50 years living here, our three children launched successfully, and friends and family welcomed to bed and table for many decades, I figured we had already gotten more than full value for our original low investment.

So, walking my talk about affordable housing, I wished to offer it back to the community at reasonable rents through a non-profit organization—particularly for performing artists.

As an artist myself, I know how hard it is for creative people to make a living doing what we do best; I love that my studio will continue being used as a space for rehearsals and classes, and that our old 'brown-shingle' will continue to be home to gifted artists.

That's what makes sense to me these days as we go through these hard times: finding sanctuary with one another, providing safe places to make art and learning how to live together.

That's what the live wire Nigerian poet Bayo Akomolafe says, too. When I first met him at a lecture and discussion he presented here a few years ago, he asked if he could be my son, after I spoke up with a comment that intrigued him!

I was sure it meant I'd been talking too much, so I just made a wry face.

"May I call you Mother? I'm serious!" he insisted with laughing eyes.

I returned the tease. "Okay, but does that mean I can scold you when you get too outrageous?"

Without missing a beat he slapped his knee and exclaimed, "My natural mother would honor you for it!"

I've since learned that it is not uncommon for young Nigerian men to take on multiple 'mothers' wherever they go.

Recently, Bayo, my new 'son' sent out a short piece to his followers about how we might all respond to fascism. It contains this:

> *As the surface congeals into fascist arrangements, and as hate and fear get codified into law, there is yet one place to go: beneath the surface. A catabasis into the under-realms. Into the folds of thick time. Into the creases of our long bodies, populated by a strange multitude. Into the fellowship of trees and the nonhuman world. Into the deep biospheres of life-death. Into dreams upon which the hieroglyphics of other worlds are faintly inscribed. Into the embrace of new questions, the asking of which is not possible when we stand on the surface of things. Into sanctuary.*

And he knows about going under the surface, which he had to do in Zaire/Congo as a boy, where his father held a government post and the family was hunted down by 'hulking soldiers' before they were ordered to find their way back to Nigeria.

So I think a lot about how we find sanctuary when the world spins crazily out of control around us, and our friends and family, as well as ourselves, stumble and fall. How do we live our one wild and precious life well, despite the obstacles? How do we protect one another and try to use the situation we are in to reach higher, live stronger, love more deeply?

How do we not give up on ourselves?

I keep coming back to the two young Croatian cellists who have appeared out of nowhere, it seems, becoming a rare gift of heart-stopping beauty and fun that is taking the world by storm.

Along with hundreds of thousands of others, I cannot go a day without listening to their music on YouTube. I'd say I was addicted to that level of beauty, now that I have experienced it, that frequency of vibration that I am now entraining to along with more and more people in the world.

These two young musicians seem to know just what they are doing, and why, as they pour out their rich soul music for us.

They play to packed arenas all over the world, and people come in families, with babies and Grandmas, all mesmerized by the music. There is something for everyone, and millions watch them on You-Tube. They are raising our vibrations song by song so that we can find sanctuary with one another *way above* the radar, not below it. They make us feel blessed while we dive with them into the rare waters they swim in.

Psychedelic Bach, I call it, whether they are playing Acid Rock or Rhianna or Bach Double Concerti—they dig deep down into the soul of the rich sanctuary of sound we all share.

That is where my hope lies, with the Bayos from Nigeria and the Lucas and Stjepans from Croatia and all the women running for office in America—the young ones we've barely noticed before who may be able to pull us all back from the brink with their great hearts and genius.

I'm *with* them! I am with them just as I am with the mysterious masterpieces appearing in fields of grain all around the world that we call 'crop circles.'

All deserve our attention!

Just as I am with eight month-old Rylan whose eyes lead me in towards the sweet wisdom of new life, while he is still so close to the source-country from whence he came; and I am with the Earth that, despite all we have done to her, still knows how to turn on her axis and create trees and grasses and flowers—and us.

(And also knows how to kick us off if She has to.)

Like it or not, we are all in this together, sanctuary for one another.

It is true, there is no time for anything but love, no matter what! Pass it on …

In this Together

When I was 19 and a student in France, I lived with a wonderful family as part-time nanny for their five children. One time, when the parents went off to Paris for a few days and left me in charge of their brood, Patrick, the three-year-old, came down with a fever and I had to call in the doctor who lived near the old church.

The children and I gathered around the burning *petit Pat*, holding our breaths while the doctor examined him.

"He is going to live," he assured us with a twinkle, "but you have to place a suppository in his anus twice a day to bring down his fever."

M le docteur did not demonstrate how to do this, assuming that the American nanny knew how to find Patrick's anus and what to do with a suppository once she found it. He left me with a bag of little waxy buttons and told me to let him know in the morning how Patrick was doing.

I was scared out of my wits, unwilling to confess my ignorance to any of them, and with no choice but to pretend efficiency at inserting suppositories into little kids' bottoms. So I took a deep breath, found the opening not at all where I expected it to be, and pushed the slippery little button in.

You may think this trite, but that was a watershed moment in my life, as I had discovered that I was capable of more than I had thought I was, even when I had no idea what I was doing. None of the children, including Patrick, ever guessed at my dilemma.

Either the ability to rise to the occasion is built-in and we all share it, or I got assistance from the angels that day, but however it happened, I quickly became a deft inserter of suppositories. Patrick recovered, of course, and I won high praise from the other children when their parents came home.

It has happened many times over the years that I've found myself stuck one way or another, but then assistance has appeared from out of nowhere, as if I had invisible guides who believed in me. I have learned to trust those guides—trust the universe, really—and am now familiar with the *feeling* I get in my body when I am offered help by unseen presences that apparently care very much for my welfare. It has happened too many times for me to doubt its reality.

I often call it 'synchronicities.'

Years ago, when Herb and I and our kids were coming back home after our yearlong sojourn in India, I had to say a tearful goodbye to my bamboo flute teacher, Sachdev. We were both in our late twenties, had bonded as friends—as family, really—and sorry to be ending our deep connection.

On our last night together, he confessed his wish to perform and teach in America. His family was forcing him to join the family construction business as an accountant, he explained with a dramatic roll of the eyes, "but if I do not play music I will die!"

We were well matched for high drama, and tearfully I promised to try, even knowing the impossibility of what he was asking me to do.

I was a busy young mother, knew nobody in the music business in the States, and had some idea of what the competition was like in my country. For well over a year back home, I simply felt guilty for not even trying to come through for him.

Then one morning I woke up knowing it was time to try, so I phoned the local Public Radio station, told them I had a reel-to-reel tape of a wonderful North Indian bass flutist, and would they play it on the air?

"Oh my God!" was the reply. "Our 11 o'clock show never came in and we've been racing around trying to find a replacement! Can you come right down to the Studio?"

So I did. I was asked to introduce him to the radio audience, mention that he was looking for a way to perform in America, tell them my phone number—and then with minutes to spare, I was on the air!

It so happened that the night before, at a Board meeting of the Ali Akbar College of Music, Fred Bower was charged with the task of looking for a teacher of North Indian flute, and the next morning he *happened* to turn on the radio at 11 o'clock.

"I never listen to the radio at that time!" he told me later. But he phoned me in excitement, we contacted Sachdev by telegram, the arrangements were made and the deed done with utter simplicity in the space of one day.

Each one of us was shell-shocked for a week.

Magic happens—all the time. I cannot say how it happens, I only know from personal experience that it does.

All I had to do was to follow some internal urge, based on nothing but trust, and follow through step by simple step until the outcome happened, as if by itself. Whether this trust was for the Universe or for myself I will never know, but several weeks later Sachdev arrived, and Fred and I went to pick him up at the airport.

And the rest is history.

So here's where I stand these days on the dire subjects we are all facing: environmental disaster; political hysteria; insane wars; racism; economy out of control:

I categorically refuse to be swamped by despair, horrific and terrifying as the situation is. Even if the worst comes to the worst, right this minute I am alive and I will not throw away one moment of my life if I can help it!

I want every second of intense feelings, whether they are the profound sorrows of loss or the creative ecstasies of love. I want to know the tangy smell of a freshly sliced lemon, and the droplet of dew on a fig leaf at dawn. I want to see delight on the face of a child when I enter the room, and know intimately the pangs of sorrow we are all facing together.

One of these days I will die, but today I am alive and I will live it!

Actually, that is how I know not to panic—the fact that I will soon be dying. We all will, every last one of us, no exceptions, and we are programmed to do so. Our towns and cities will do so as well, and every one of our friends and relatives, wherever they live.

Our cultures will change and the seas will engulf the lands, and the ice sheets will cover the planet, as they have many times before, and whole civilizations will disappear from the face of the earth until the cycle shifts yet again.

If you believe that there is a part of us that continues on even after our bodies die, then there is no reason to panic. I am one of those believers, as it happens, having learned to be after sitting at bedside after bedside of dying friends, and being witness to the effulgent joy on their faces as each one passed.

They showed me, in their last moments, seeing what all the ancient traditions confirm—that there is more to this world than we have been taught, and death is simply one transition of many.

So we can relax our fear of dropping invisibly off the edge of the world, for there is no such thing.

What is happening to us and our world is not a new phenomenon, and there is nowhere to go but here—a rather larger and more-dimensioned 'Here' than we think—so we might as well face the reality and relax.

So eat, drink and be merry!

Who was it who said that?

Well, I agree.

Midnight's Children

Yesterday morning the sun never rose. When I awoke, the world was still at bruised midnight, as if fire had darkened the sun—which it had. We learned later that the smoke from the fires burning across the Western seaboard were trapped high up by a cloud layer beneath it, shutting out our source of light and turning day into night.

It felt mythic, like a twilight of the Gods.

And smelled like Death.

Götterdämmerung this has been called, an old story of chaotic world-altering destruction featuring madmen in power, violence in the streets, fires out of control and dark skies in the morning. It is about chaos and cataclysm leading to massive destruction, followed by an eventual emergence into a new and more richly dimensioned reality.

I believe this may be the current stage of a series of shifts of consciousness that have been happening in the world for a long time now, much longer than our particular lifetimes. It has been a tough curriculum that has included courses in male domination and private ownership of the Earth, colonizing of indigenous populations and religious wars defining God narrowly and meanly. It seems clear that a big changeover is in process, and is inevitable in our human story if life is to survive on our planet!

Who would ever have guessed the number of horror stories all taking place simultaneously, though? We've got everything from pandemics and wildfires to wars and racial madness … take a breath … also fascism and skewed elections and massive Unidentified Flying Objects hovering over the Kremlin and the White House seen by thousands for hours, but unreported by the media! (I'm not making this up!)

All—and more—at the same time!

I do not believe this has much to do with Democrats and Republicans, but is something *much* bigger!

So now what do we do?

Yesterday was awful; the air was putrid and I gave way to despair, sheltering in place alone, frightened and bored. I needed to walk off my mood, sob out my grief in a beloved friend's arms, yell out my story (along with everyone else in the world, I wager) but all that was verboten, so I ate a gritty lunch and swiped away at the ants invading my kitchen and stamped my feet when my mouse showed herself!

Little smartasses!

Then I remembered that long-ago day in Oxford when I was 23 years old, newly married and reading a novel that, in fact, set the course for my life. It was *Le Dernier des Justes—The Last of the Just*—by the French author Andre Schwarz-Bart, about a good man in Germany during the horrors of the Nazi era.

I sat reading in the kitchen beneath a single lightbulb in the early dusk of a winter's afternoon—winter nights fall early in England—and was curled up close to the electric heater and waiting for Herb to come home from the Math Institute. I recall the smell of brussels sprouts and chestnuts cooking on the stove, and the ticking of our clock as I was nearing the final scene in the book, which takes place in a gas chamber.

This good, 'just man' has been protecting the children in the camp, listening to them and loving them. On the last page of the book, they are taken into the gas chamber together and the door shuts with a clang behind them. Opening his arms, he brings them all into his embrace, starting to sing as the gas jets are turned on.

"Sing with me ..." he entreats the children, "Sing, my little lambs. Breathe quickly ..."

Respirez vite, mes agneaux ..." is how the book ends.

Collapsing onto the floor of the kitchen myself, I was sobbing helplessly, inconsolably curled around the electric heater. Luckily, Herb arrived a short time later, and he found me there, in a smoke-filled room, my gum-soled shoes melting in the heat of the electric fire and me helplessly weeping on the kitchen floor.

First he eased off my smoking shoes and tossed them into the kitchen sink, and then held and rocked me while I sobbed, although he had no idea what I was crying about.

It was hours before I could tell him because, as a Holocaust survivor himself when he was three years old, he could easily have been one of those children.

I made a pledge that night that no matter what was to happen in my lifetime, however frightening, I would honor the memory of that man by continuing his work, reassuring and giving comfort wherever I could.

I would "sing to the children," offering safety and laughter—in however many forms that took—as my life's work.

That was a long time ago, late on a dark and rainy afternoon during our honeymoon year in England, an actual train ride away from where those atrocities had in fact happened not very long before.

That is why I write these little pieces and send them out every two weeks to anybody who asks to receive them.

Just today I overheard someone say, "... find the wounds and turn them into wisdom ..." before I walked beyond hearing range. Yes, I thought, that makes sense, and that takes patience.

Do I have that kind of patience?

Just now my little mouse scurried across the room right under my nose and stopped and looked back at me for a moment, as if to say,

"Here I am! Do you still love me … ?"

All I can do is laugh.

Yes, I do, is my answer.

The Dachau Stone

Since the trip Herb and I made to Germany in the early sixties, to visit the house and neighborhood where he was born in Aachen, I have never wished to return to that country. In fact, our week there was so traumatizing for me that we had to cut the time short and take an early morning train out for Paris, at my insistence. I didn't breathe easily until we were well beyond the border—the same border he had crossed escaping out of when he was two years old.

Herb didn't have that reaction, though. He could have stayed longer, done more exploring, visited the new city of Berlin and, in fact, he has gone back a number of times over the years for scientific meetings. Each time, he has taken a tram out to one of the local concentration camps, bearing witness and pondering the imponderable past.

He arrives home shaken each time, still barely able to understand the reality of what took place there, and each time re-commits to the country that provided haven for his family when they were refugees. During his last visit, some 20 years ago, he brought back for me a stone from the concentration camp at Dachau that he picked up off the ground, and with it, a poem he had written in a local café that night:

This stone I give to you,
Symbol of the ashes of that most awful place,
We too, but for God's grace.
Life and love more precious to contemplate
Seen hanging by the gossamer thread of Fate!

For all these years, the stone and the poem have been on my altar in the studio, tucked in the back where only I can see it. My idea was that whatever energy of evil still lurked in that bit of stone might gradually be cleansed out through the love and healing work happening in my dance studio day after day, year after year.

Periodically, I have taken it out and held it in my palm, feeling for that stinging sensation I have come to recognize as sickness. For years I could still feel it there, but the sting grew fainter as time went on. When I meditated with it recently the stone felt clean, a simple bit of rock again, and I knew it was time to return it to the earth where it belongs.

We lit a *Yahrtzeit* candle last night and leaned the stone against the glass before we went to bed.

It is Mothers' Day today, and we went down to the Bay for a quiet hour together, the stone in my pocket until the right moment to give it over to the water. Herb held it for awhile, and then spoke about letting it go, but not forgetting its significant story; I then took it and spoke directly to it, asking it, now that its vibration has been raised after all these years of healing balm, to please help us as we try to shift human consciousness from fear and willful evil to kindness and self-assured intelligence.

"However small you are, your help is needed," I whispered to the stone. "Please."

And then I climbed down the breakwater rocks, got as close to the water as I could without falling, tested the strong west wind to make sure the stone wouldn't get tossed back in my face, lifted my throwing arm and aimed for the waves. It hit the water with a small, unobtrusive plunk and sank immediately.

A story of more than half a century, more lives held in the balance than we can imagine, and the Dachau stone was gone.

I hope it will do its work.

While I was writing this, Julius came to the door—Julius who has been coming to our door for almost as long as the Dachau stone has been sitting on my altar. Homeless, he has lived beneath a freeway underpass surviving harsh winters, diabetes, incurable poverty and a spirit that just won't quit. He is 80 now, he claims, still gets around on a bike, has no teeth left but carries a worn out broom with which he offers to sweep our sidewalk.

I have gotten to know him over the years, so I am familiar with his story. His life has been unspeakably hard, but he is a survivor with a sense of humor. More often than not, we give him money—for insulin, he claims—but he never accepts food. Sometimes he comes too often—twice in a week—and I tell him that he cannot always count on us; there are times when, for our own reasons, we will not answer the door. Ignoring him without surging guilt is difficult for me, but today has to be one of those days as it is about our own past horrors, our day to remember—our day to slough off a long-held burden and give it to the sea.

It also is Mothers' Day and having been daughter, wife, mother and grandmother in turn, I need to take stock. Today I must take a deep breath and consider what is mine to receive, and what is mine to give. And when.

But it is not easy...

... Life and love more precious to contemplate
Seen hanging by the gossamer thread of Fate!

We too but for God's grace...

Decoding Donald

When I was in my mid teens and living in Queens, New York, there were two Donalds around, one I knew and the other I didn't. Donald McKayle was my modern dance teacher and the other Donald was a kid who lived in our neighborhood and went to the same High School as my brother before getting kicked out for being an intractable bully.

His name was Donald Trump.

Reading the memoir by Mary Trump about her life growing up in the extended Trump family—*Too Much and Not Enough*—I find myself in spookily familiar territory. That world still resides in my bones, and my neighbors, mostly second-generation immigrants from Europe, still haunt my dreams. They were mostly Italians, Irish and Germans—and the Russian Jews like us who had come over from the old country just one generation earlier. Our parents were desperate to prosper as Americans after the horrors and deprivations of the Second World War and the deadly 'Bomb,' and humor was in short supply. Many of them, still broken by the trauma of growing up poor with frightened parents who barely spoke English, worked hard to prove themselves good Americans who could provide well for their families, whatever it took. Some were better at it than others.

In my family, the men were a desperate lot and the women were furious behind their fur coats. My father pretended to be rich, but wasn't. He was deep into a debt he kept secret from us until he died before his 50th birthday, leaving us with his piled-up debts behind him. Our particular story of hidden poverty and shame was probably not all that unusual, and maneuvering around the law was certainly not uncommon. Papa Trump did it successfully, it seems, racking up his millions by sleight of hand and sitting on huge properties and influence in the boroughs of New York.

His oldest son, Freddy, refused the position of being groomed for his father's empire, paid dearly for his attempt at independence and died much too young, penniless and alcoholic. That left Donald, the next male offspring in the family in the position to receive the gifts of money and property, making him the major heir to the family fortune.

In my mind I walk those streets again, a wraith from another world quite out of place where I lived. Everything about it rang false to me, and I soaked in the pathos, wishing I were somebody else's daughter somewhere far away. I longed to dance, but was not allowed to for reasons I never quite understood, although I eventually forced the issue by making my own money babysitting and taking classes with Donnie McKayle when I could slip away.

For the most part I lay low, kept an eye out for my younger siblings and kept my own counsel, and remained more or less intact on the inside. On the outside I was an utter failure—all but flunking out of school, unable to tame my thick black hair and not finding a boyfriend who had any idea what I was talking about.

At night in bed, in my imagination I danced and dreamed of brilliance.

The Queens County of the 1950s was rapidly sprouting with suburbs and housing projects when we arrived there from Brooklyn, part of the first generation after the one 'off the boat,' as my parents would say. These Housing Developments—which would make Donald's wheeler and dealer father a multi-millionaire—was the place many European immigrants *moved up* to from their first entry points into this country after Ellis Island a generation earlier.

My family was part of this exodus, along with the German Jews fleeing the Holocaust. We mostly kept to our own kind, even in the great mixing pot of the public schools, but my favorite neighbors were the Italians across the street and the old Polish couple who grew tomatoes and carrots in their yard despite being pitied because they 'couldn't afford canned.' My best friend was the Rabbi's daughter whose family came from Ukraine, and I was shy around her cultured parents, so different from mine.

Every weekday morning, the men took the Subway trains to work in 'the city,' and the women stayed home to keep house, play *mahjong* and take care of the children. On the weekends, I barely knew whose Dad was whose. The world I knew was comprised of women and children, except for the guy who drove the bus and a gang of teenage boys known as the Black Hawks.

This pattern was true for the Trump family as well; Papa, a fiercely ambitious man, worked 12 hour days to make his millions (by whatever means, apparently) and Mama, a recent immigrant from an island off the coast of Scotland, stayed home to cook and take care of their children. With her last child, while Donald was still a toddler, she became ill enough to take to her bed and the two youngest were left mostly in the care of nannies. From then on, apparently acting out in rage for the mother-love he was missing, he became a kid impossible to control.

Donald and I both grew up in this world of frustrated women and men dreaming of riches, scheming how to get their share. None of us young folks seemed to have any idea what was going on in the grown-up world, nor did we tend to talk about our parents with our friends. Some of us, like me, went silent and some, like Donald, made sure they got noticed by being either brilliant or Bad. My brother says he was constantly getting into trouble in school until he finally got himself kicked out and sent off to a Military Academy.

I took off for France as soon as I was old enough to run, feeling guilty I wasn't sticking around to protect my brother and sister; Donald moved up the family ladder, feeding off Papa's money until he resided in a golden tower in New York City, turning tricks and deals he continued to get away with.

… And the rest is history.

Mary Trump tells the family story in detail from her point of view as Donald's niece, including the story of her father Freddy's tragic death at the age of 42, describing the funeral parlor and the shock of his loss in vivid detail. It was especially vivid to me because my father also died before he was 50 and we were also in full shock. I could swear, from her descriptions, that the funeral parlor her father was laid out in was the same one my father was laid out in when he died.

I suspect, though, that our Russian-Jewish family created a lot more ruckus there than the Trump family did, as my great-aunt arrived late and barged into the wrong room, yelling for my father! We heard her laments through the walls, her unmistakable hoarse Yiddish coming through loud and clear as she terrified the astounded grieving family next door! It took four of us—her two sons, Herb and me—to rush to the rescue and man-handle her out of there and into the right room where she started all over again, wailing at top voice and staggering towards the open casket to throw herself in on top of my father, beseeching him to wake up and drive her home!

As Donald currently outdoes himself in outrageousness, I remember Aunt Clara and wonder which family wins the prize for outrageous behavior. I'd say, though, that my great-aunt came by her madness honestly, having been born in the generation that fled persecution in Russia, dodging Cossaks who burned down whole villages, raping all the women and slaughtering the men. My great-grandmother escaped by literally running away with her four young daughters hidden beneath her wide skirts. Somehow they made their way to the boat that would get them to America—but the story does not end there, since they were turned back at Ellis Island because one of the sisters had glaucoma! So they had to return to the Old Country and more *pogroms,* and try again a few years later! Eventually they all made it out of there and onto American soil, but not one of the sisters ever quite recovered either physically or mentally.

Not too surprising.

I come from a line of very crazy heroines who came by their madness honestly! The men hardly stood a chance. The Yiddish word for such women is *balleboste.* For Donald's family, I cannot speak.

My forebears were desperate people longing for life. Donald's forebears also must have been, even those who tried to be good Nazi soldiers a generation earlier. In any case, money was a way to put that all behind them and be 'someone,' however it was come by. Power was a way to be someone, however it was come by and both madness and fraud in such pursuits were not uncommon, as you might expect. They still aren't.

But I'm looking for the silver lining here, the place of hope where we all long to be whether we know it or not. I'm searching for an example of the radical resilience that arises when all the chips are down, and things seem at their bleakest but we find a way, anyhow. I know it has to exist!

It does! In fungi.

It turns out that mushrooms in nuclear accident zones have increased melanin and grow dark! The melanin not only detoxifies the toxic radioactive waste, but also *benefits* it and the surviving life forms around it!

Change!

For example, in the 'Exclusion Zone' in the area surrounding Chernobyl, after the horrific meltdown of its nuclear power plant over 30 years ago, the ecosystem has rebounded into a natural wildlife refuge for native species, some not seen there in centuries. There are bison, moose, lynx, boars, wolves, dogs, birds, insects …

Some scientists conclude, perhaps tongue in cheek, that for some animals, humans may be more dangerous than radioactivity!

This ability to not only overcome adversity, but also to use it to grow stronger in some unexpected direction, is now called 'radical resilience' and is a testament to Life's ability to not only heal, but to grow stronger after having to deal with adversity. The tougher the curriculum, the more creative we get. That's our work, I wager, getting burned until we figure out how to use the fire in ways we've not yet dreamed of.

And there's a kid from my old neighborhood out there who is pushing us in that direction, whether he means to or not. We can fight him, sure, but some of us can use that energy to get creative and make some big changes that have been needing attention for a very long time. It may be now or never.

If the puppies in Chernobyl can do it, why not us?

Getting Real

The way you prepare a sheep for slaughter is to praise her, kiss her pointy face and tell her how glad you've been to know her, weep while she eats the treat of oats you've offered her—and then lead her out to the pasture where the stun gun awaits.

Daisy knew something was up and she resisted mightily, but we pulled her forward to where Adrien and the rest of the team awaited us, and they took over. We held on hard while the deed was done in two quick motions of a stun-gun and sharp knife. She fell, bleeding, at our feet.

It took less than a minute.

We were seven adults and five children in the goat meadow, and we drew together, arms around one another for comfort, and I noticed that even the youngest of the children did not look away. It seemed as though they sensed how important it was to know about how the real world worked, even when it was hard to look at.

They had a million questions—so did I—and Adrien calmly answered each one in his Albanian-accented English, while he separated bone from bone, slit skin and prepared what only moments before had been 'Daisy,' and was now something to be skinned and eventually eaten.

Hanging the carcass upside down from a tree-limb, Adrien gave four of us adults each a small, sharp knife and demonstrated how to skin the carcass by pulling the fleece slowly downwards and gently stroking away at the connective tissue between skin and pink flesh. Working together, shoulder to shoulder, we were so absorbed in our task it was easy to forget that only moments before we had accompanied Daisy, on her own feet, to this place.

Before slitting the belly to release the organs, we set up buckets to catch them and we asked Adrien to name each organ as it slid out.

"This is a kidney," he announced, holding up a small purplish blob surrounded by fat, "… and here's the intestines in this sac. See the heart here? And there's the gall bladder, watch, don't slit it because it will stink, and the liver—it's big, no? …"

It took less than an hour before the carcass was totally skinned and eviscerated, hanging upside down and ready to be butchered.

When the empty carcass was laid on a waiting table, we asked Adrien to identify for us the cuts of 'meat' as he butchered the body into chops and tenderloin, stew meat and leg of lamb. The children began to disperse to the hammock to play and for the next few hours the adults cleaned up, shared cuts of meat to take home with them or to put into the freezer on the farm. Adrien claimed all the fat and Brent brought the ribs to his yurt for a barbeque and invited everyone down to his place later that night for spicy ribs.

When it was time to bury the offal, Hannah from the Black Banjo Reclamation Project combed through the small intestines to harvest the thinnest strands for banjo strings, and the rest was brought down the hill to the stream, where the coyotes howl late in the night.

Not a morsel of what had been Daisy was wasted.

Later, the sizzle of lamb fat on the grill drew us down to Brent's place where we gathered around the spit and tasted the meat for the first time—all of us. Daisy would now become part of everyone who had known her in life and witnessed her death; we were now all kin, part of one another—literally.

I believe that looking straight at life and death is something we all will have to do as we move into an unknown future on this planet. We'll have to face some hard realities, knowing we need one another to survive, and always have.

To provide the food we grow on our farm-in-the-city requires a whole community of people each doing his and her share of the work, and the sun and healthy soil and regular rainfall and the bees all in balance, together. It requires that we know each other well enough to live and work together, to feel admiration for each of our particular gifts and a willingness to trust one another, since we create a much stronger fabric, together, than if each of us is a separate strand, competing with the others for what we all need.

I was moved by how strongly we bonded doing the work of providing for the community together. No money passed hands, but by the end of the day we felt even stronger as a group, having taken life so that we all might live during the next six months. We had gone through a painful, but necessary process together; I figure it was practice for the challenge everyone on the planet is facing now, as the end point of our outdated civilization becomes more evident.

Either we shift some of our old assumptions about how the world works, or it could be curtains for all of us: old assumptions that presume a competitive economy that sets us one against the other; that winners take all, and that the earth can be sold to the highest bidder.

After well over 2000 years of being taught that such notions were the 'truth,' we are at the brink of a major shift of mindset we may have to fight for. And you and I are the ones who have to make the radical transition, every one of us!

It is that change of consciousness we have been born for, I believe; we are the ones we've been waiting for—and now, right NOW is the time!

I do not expect it will be easy, but the old story is over, whoever takes this election—it's just a matter of time.

We've all been traumatized for centuries and have been nursed on the fear residing in our mothers' milk. It is an old, old story of enforced trepidation: that we need to be afraid of one another because if *you* have enough, there will not be enough for me, and if everything is a contest, I have to be a winner and not a loser.

Whole societies have been based on this model of separation that raises some of us high and lowers the rest to 'workers.' Unfortunately, the natural world is considered to be in the 'worker' category, meaning that those of us with enough power and money can buy and own it, and do with it whatever we wish, including destroying it!

Imagine!

What will it take for our consciousness to evolve and recognize that we are all in this together, through life and death, playing our roles side by side with one another and learning how to listen to the larger music we make together?

I remember the time, many years ago, when I sat in on a rehearsal of a Schubert string quartet in which the second violinist was my boyfriend, and when the quartet reached a strong, final chord, the woman sitting next to me leaned over and whispered,

"Who's the best player?"

I believe I answered, "They all are."

At least I hope I did.

Cleaning Up the Mess

Waking up this morning to the election news, I feel like a mountain climber who has dragged herself to what she thought was the mountaintop, only to discover she had just reached a pile of rocks along the way. There is still a long trek before the true summit, but she's all but run out of food, her thick boots are in shreds and her companions are weary. She badly needs to rest, but they dare not stop.

For some reason this brings out all my instincts for cleaning house, to straighten things up so I can see what I still have to do and how I have come to be where I am.

Here on the farm that makes literal sense, as we're still dealing with the leftover debris from our big retrofit project. We've moved in, but the house is still surrounded by the last piles of bricks, torn-up concrete and the occasional old appliance; frankly, it looks like a junkyard. One day soon, we tell one another, we'll do the final clean-up and turn this place into the stunning demonstration of green building it is meant to be.

This morning I realized we have unwittingly created a metaphor for the world right now: we've made a mess and now we have to try and clean it up. How do we even start?

My guess is we have to go way back in time, back to first causes thousands of years ago, after the long eras of Ice Ages and Floods when the survivors were finding their way back to dry land. When I look as far back as I can and try to imagine myself as one of those survivors, I notice that the most precious thing in my world is something hidden in plain sight—the Earth itself. Herself. The land is our home and mother and provider and Goddess. Upon Her our very life depends and we want to 'own' her, stake a claim on some part of her that becomes our 'property' that we will defend with our very lives.

I believe the issue may be that basic—and that ancient.

It is ridiculous, of course, to think that we can 'own' the Earth, especially given that few of us live more than ten decades at the most, but the idea is ingrained somewhere in our psyches that those who own land will survive; those who do not, will perish, although most indigenous societies remained small enough to coexist upon shared land, recognizing that their lives were inextricably connected with its health and balance.

'Landlords' are relatively new in the scheme of things. Lords of Land? I mean, really? Then when you link that up with money and a class system, you must really be confused! So then when you add racial slavery and fossil fuels and rape of the land and of women, you know you've gotten desperately off the track!

That's sort of where we are now. So how do we find our way back? (Other than, of course, having a contest between two teams represented by an elephant and a donkey bashing each other to Hell and back!)

Dismantling a broken-down old ranch house, we discovered, meant a whole lot more than just tearing out old wiring and patching up broken window frames. Each layer of rot revealed the next layer of rot until we were down to the floor joists and the accumulation of rat poop and toxic dirt in the ancient crawl space. Almost everything had

170

to go, much of it dug out by hand and our faces covered by masks long before everyone else was wearing them!

Yuck-a-muck! I wondered what in the world we had gotten ourselves into! Maybe we should have just closed the door and let it be, but in fact there was no going back. The process of transformation was underway, like it or not, and we had to see it through for better or for worse—though nobody ever said transformation was easy.

The natural world does it all the time, recycling and transforming one form into another. On the Galápagos, I remember coming upon a dead sea lion on the shore of Isla Santiago, crawling with maggots and flapping seabirds coming down to feed. We came back the next day to find the body stripped down to bare bones, the dead sea lion having been transformed overnight into food for a myriad of other living creatures.

Down to bare bones. We may need to do some version of that ourselves—strip down our assumptions, recall the basics of living systems of which we are a part, redefine how we shall live upon this Earth and with one another.

If not now, then when? If not us, then who?

I mean, what else is there for us to do during lock-down?

Darkness Before Dawn

Breakfast this morning was my usual—leftovers from the night before—which today was a stew of veggies over rice, onions, red peppers and garlic, a delicious way to start the day. As my mouth registered the layered rings of onion, the clove shapes of garlic buds and the curves of roasted pepper, my mind subtly spread into their vegetable lives. I felt their growth in soil, their forming into bulbs and flowers, their responses to sunlight and rain. I was green along with them as their lives and deaths became part of the taste of breakfast.

Hard to describe, but it felt like my whole being spread out past my skin to encompass the whole world and time, turning my simple breakfast into a holy act.

I actually cried, grateful nobody was around to witness my epiphanies over breakfast!

After all these months of quarantine and slowed-down living I am becoming a monk, increasingly more aware of the subtle dimensions of ordinary things hidden in plain sight—new ones every day. It's like slowly inching my way up one side of a see-saw, feeling the board slowly balance beneath my legs as I edge towards the middle. The tipping point. In a moment, the whole thing will shift and go *bonk!*

Like the world.

As I see it, now is the time to pivot, shift our weight and balance in a new place, or we'll fall off. Time to prepare for the future, not pine for the past. Can we do it?

Something we cannot yet name is changing, like a child in the womb preparing to be born. She grows slowly out of sight for months of slow preparation, and then dramatically pushes her way through into the air of the world. Huge contractions happen, and blood and searing pain, fear and single-minded strength are needed for her to get born, nothing less. And then all is changed as we find ourselves in a new place out beyond the enclosure we had assumed for nine months was the edge of home.

For life to continue, the baby has to grow up or die. It's that simple. It is end of an era; it is the beginning of an era.

Lately, a teacher has come to take up residence in my little studio home, showing me how to take on the challenges of life in a changing, world—a field mouse, in fact.

He is brilliant; I cannot outsmart him no matter how hard I try! At first I considered him an unwelcome intruder, but as we get to know each other, I am awed by his cunning.

Believe me, he is a lot smarter than I am! Some mornings, after he has foiled my attempts to keep him on his own side of the wall, he will pop up in full sight on the bookcase by my bed, and we stare with curiosity at each other. He *sees* me, reads my every blink. Who knew mice were so smart?

"How do you do this?" I whispered one morning, "I closed up every hole last night."

I swear he shot me a grin.

The new hole, perfectly round, was actually four feet off the ground by the electric wall socket in the kitchen! "But *how?*" I asked out loud.

I must have shrugged with too much energy because he took off in a quick minute, and was gone.

A few days ago I got to watch Mia the goat give birth to her twins in the barn. Her sides heaved and she backed into the wall of the manger for support as two tiny hoofs with a little pink nose between them emerged from her straining body. I remembered what it felt like to give birth myself, spreading impossibly wide to bring new life into the world—and how much it hurt! It was helpless and power-filled, impossible and ordained, triumphant and exhausted. All of that, and more.

As this new life slid bloodily into the hay of the manger, we held our breaths as the baby goat breathed in its first gulping breath. And tried to stand on wobbly little legs, making tinny little bleats while its mother licked its wet, furry body with a tongue that knew what to do, even though she had never done it before.

I could feel again the wonderment of those first moments when your baby breathes on his own, your womb is emptied of its perfectly-formed new person and your life is inexorably changed forever.

Your life is reset. New life is here, and is dependent on you to survive. You have no choice but to rise to the occasion, but there is nothing else you would rather be doing as your whole being commits to the charge in love because life is changed now—forever. And the task is yours, no matter what.

The task is *ours*, no matter what! Starting *now!*

Heresy and the Holy Grail

for Gary, Peter, Faisal and Bridget

It has been called 'the Holy Grail,' the hitherto unattainable golden cup or ancient book or secret bloodline, sought but never found, precious beyond imagining. Nobody knew from whence this mysterious 'something' came, nor what it represented, nor how to find it, but we humans have been searching for it everywhere for millennia, without ever quite knowing what we were looking for.

Who knows, perhaps it is right here, right now, hidden in plain sight right under our noses for us to recognize; we just have to know how to look.

I think I had an inkling of a Holy Grail the other night at an intimate concert given by some friends. The venue was on the upper floor of a clapboard house down by the railroad tracks, where excellent music happens frequently in what is more of a crowded living room than a concert hall. The impresario, an unassuming fellow who built this room for music and believes in the gift economy, turns over all the ticket proceeds to the musicians.

On this night they were an ensemble of four people I have known for years who play on stringed gourds and drums from Macedonia,

Greece, Bulgaria and Turkey, improvising on traditional melodies and performing their own compositions based on those same soulful scales. Their improvisations were daring and seamless and they teased the melodies, challenging one another to subtler and richer depths of sound and rhythm created in the moment.

In the soft, delicate passages we had to hold our breaths or we'd miss the music, and when they took off, the whole place shook!

Oh, it was grand!

My whole body became a listening instrument, feeling the music even more than hearing it. It was as if my skin got filled to bursting with sound and my heart brimmed all the way over into tears. In those moments I knew things I had not known even an hour before I'd walked in the door, truths too deep for words and sensations too stunning for even laughter.

I knew—the way we sometimes know things—that I had stepped into a province in which all of reality was encompassed, whole and beautiful. Life and death were there in equal measure and the universe was glorious beyond description, an alchemical pairing of every quality imaginable: good and evil, light and dark; male and female; earth and spirit.

The music touched the ineffable, it was the joy that passeth all understanding, the cup that runneth over, the immediate knowing that the Universe is magnificent and balanced and good, and that it works in mysterious ways.

Not a golden goblet, but Grail-like enough for me!

In other times I would have been declared a heretic, daring to have this level of spiritual experience on my own without benefit of ordained clergy. (Ordained by whom, one might ask?) I would have been hunted down as a witch, burned at the stake, thrown to hungry beasts. The Holy Orders would have declared me anathema.

For centuries, hundreds of thousands of both women and men—but mostly women—were punished vilely for presuming knowledge of the natural world, for celebrating the Mystery with dancing and singing, for performing mystic communion—not to mention the sexual kind— with each other and the cosmos.

And the punishment for heresy was torture and death.

The word 'heretic,' I've recently learned, comes originally from the Greek hairetikós, meaning "someone in possession of facts who is able to choose …" However, it later got re-defined as one so disobedient and wicked that he/she deserved to die a horrible and cruel death at the hands of the authorities who were, of course, in the 'right.' Whole peoples, like the Cathars in France, were wantonly rounded up and killed for thinking 'wrong.'

For centuries it was so dangerous to have knowledge in touch with the deeper Mysteries that heretics—that is, us—have had to go underground in order to stay alive.

At some point we took that to mean that books and rituals had to be hidden from ordinary people because the teachings themselves were too dangerous for the average person to practice. Considered 'esoteric,' they became secret doctrines because it was supposed that they took special powers to use safely. Only certain people could have access to Mysteries that were reserved for the initiated, the chosen few—men, mostly—who invariably wore fancy robes.

Jeez …

The Holy Grail is precious, yes, and is right before our noses and available to every one of us, costing almost nothing except for some work on our parts and the awareness that it is possible. It helps to have some supportive friends, satisfying rituals together with music and dancing, firelight and the full moon. Another approach is solitude in dark chambers, pushing us to our limits.

Plant medicine, sensory deprivation, fasting and meditation have been used, but however we do it, I believe it is our shared birthright to experience the ecstatic heights of a profound experience of the cosmos.

Last night, all it took was a cozy space generously gifted, a gathering of interested people, four brilliant musicians who loved what they were doing, and music that lifted our souls to the stars.

Simple. An impromptu Holy Grail.

One of many, I am sure.

Migrations

I have just read the following sentence in a book of stories by David James Duncan: "I've heard that migration has been defined as a bridge—a bridge that birds, animals and nomads cross as the world behind them becomes uninhabitable. A bridge that vanishes behind them as they go, leaving them no choice but the far side ..."

That speaks to me as our world becomes ever more difficult to live in, and I wonder where it might make sense to migrate to—in the world, or out of the world—to other galaxies, for example? Or are we humans supposed to stay in place and try to heal the 'home' we know, restoring it to the beauty it once had because, in fact, there's really no other world to go to other than our own?

Wherever we go, there we are ...

Years ago I spent some weeks on the south coast of Brittany, in France, living amongst the megaliths at Carnac, those mysterious alignments of massive standing stones—12 rows across—that march for miles like an army across the countryside by the sea. Sheep grazed amongst them and as, at the time it was not yet a tourist destination,

I was mostly alone wandering the ancient alignments and 'dolmens' and stone circles dotting the coast.

Day after day I walked and meditated and wrote amongst these silent witnesses to an era long gone, trying to understand what these long-ago people knew that we of the modern world had forgotten? Who were they, when had they lived here and whyever had they gone to so much trouble to place massive, shaped rocks in this place by the sea? And how come almost nobody now seemed interested?

Each day I selected three sites to visit and settled in amongst them, learning how to listen for their silent messages, taking notes and naps and following where they led me, from the snaking stone rows that went on and on, and then up the hillside to a water tower peeking out from trees. There I came upon an ancient chamber, called Kercado, hidden deep in a forest above the town on private land and I snuck in. A small notice at the dolmen-chamber told me I was welcome if I kept the site pristine

Every day after that, I found my way there either at dawn, mid-day or early evening, learning how it felt at different hours and weathers, and wondering about its history. It felt familiar, somehow, as if I had been there before. I was almost always alone there, except for a sweet white cat who often kept me company, and yet I often sensed that the stone on top of the mound was trying to say something to me, especially when I sat with my back against it.

Gradually, weird as it was, I tried to 'listen', but not with my ears, and indeed I began to gather meaning, despite myself, and the quieter and more receptive I became, the more I learned how to take in what was trying to come through.

Inside the dark chamber, alone in the utter silence, I gradually got past my own fear in the pitch darkness, and I began to relax and listen for whatever was coming through. It came as both images and feelings, sometimes ringing with a stream of sound and image like a subtle dream. It felt like my whole self—body, mind, heart, spirit—was receiving a download of information about the multi-dimensionality of the world. Swirling colors and subtle sounds showed me how all form was born of consciousness—not the other way around.

Life was a dance of being, forms in motion shot through with light, and love was the glue that held everything together. Not one thing, not one moment was left out of the Whole Thing through Time and Space and Beyond, and I was part of it All. Of course!

Even after my death. There was nothing to fear because there was nowhere else to go but here.

Living and dead, we were all right here. Infinitely. I was not ever alone, and neither was anybody else.

Emerging from the darkness of the covered mound, totally shaken each time but sensing I was supposed to be here, I would climb to the top of the dolmen and, leaning against the standing stone there I wrote down everything I could remember. As I scribbled quick notes, now in the light of day, images kept expanding in my brain like water on a thirsty plain. Emotions and sensations flowed like braided streams joining into a sheen of water sinking into dry earth and flowing underground towards an unseen sea.

I wrote down every single thing I could remember.

I realized that when I was inside the chamber, the information came to me as the receiver, but out on top I was more a transmitter of what I had received—like a radio but without the wires!

I heard the message clearly as if the stone spoke to me and the 'voice' felt female.

"It is time to let people know. You are one carrier."

Odd? Well, yes, but there it was and apparently, unbeknownst to myself, I had chosen to come to Brittany to do this task, like a transformer carrying energy and information at the right time and place, and in a language understandable to others like myself.

All I had known was that I had to go to Brittany, in France, and I went.

Anyhow, I tell this story because on my last day in Carnac, I went back to Kercado after dawn to say my last farewells to the stone I now thought of as a teacher, and alone on top of the dolmen in the early blush of morning light, facing the stone, I cried for awhile and spoke in a choking whisper, "I have to leave now but I will be back. As soon as I can, I promise."

Tears flowed, I bowed deeply (to a stone!) and immediately heard in my mind, "Absolutely not! Do not come back! This land is the old world; the new world is where you belong! That is why you were born there! Go back now! GO!"

I was shocked and have to admit that I felt a bit the over-dramatic fool, but by the time I cycled back into town I took the admonition seriously, canceled the next leg of my trip to Glastonbury, took the afternoon train to Paris and flew home as soon as I could book a flight.

I have never gone back.

I stand by the information, and the subtle warnings I heard during those weeks about the major changes we would all soon be witnessing, and that we had to hold on and learn from everything, including our fear itself and of the coming changes we would all be experiencing. That we had been born for these times—all of us—and that our work was to accept the reality of Now, and neither reject nor fear it, but to live it well, opening willingly into the intensity of our own experiences.

But that is what life is all about—turning whatever is given to us, however terrifying, into the refining fire of our particular lives on Earth? This is ours, right now, and it has the power to turn us into gold, I believe, even if it hurts like Hell. We are the ones who were born for this time and every one of us must try and make a difference for good, recognizing it is ours to do. To not do so we would miss our opportunity to do what we came here to do—and Lord knows, every one of us is needed!

One way or another;
whoever we are;
together;
whether we believe we can;
or not.
Breathe …

A Walk in Bad Shoes

Years ago, a good friend and I hiked the cliff trail on the North Cornwall coast in England from Land's End to past Tintagel Castle—about 100 miles. It was a great adventure, though it all but destroyed me as I wore new hiking boots I'd neglected to break in before the trip. By Tintagel, my Achilles tendons were badly swollen, and I was in excruciating pain.

So, when the goats broke out of their pen the other day, and were munching away on the new greens we'd planted in the garden, I forgot about my chronic injury and ran to the rescue, stomping and yelling and chasing them down the hill.

I also forgot that goats are smarter than I am, and that they laugh at outraged humans who run after them—beh! beh! beh!—so for them this was an amusing game, and they leapt right back over the fence as I limped, with my re-inflamed heels, back up the hill.

I am a slow learner, it seems, and now I have to live again with this chronic injury and the burning pain that halts me in my tracks just when I need to be moving fast. Damn!

So I've been wondering about intelligent self-protection in these hard times; about mutual benefit; about combating the harm we inadvertently do to ourselves and one another since our competitive system encourages it.

And I think about shame.

For example, in Cornwall I could have explained to my friend that I needed a day to go inland to buy some cheap rubber sandals to save my burning feet, but I was ashamed to admit I'd been stupid enough to bring stiff new boots on a 100 mile hike! I know better, right? It wasn't the first time I had shamed myself by not paying attention to the obvious and been witnessed as a loser.

Indeed, I might have been embarrassed to request we halt our hike for a day, but no doubt we'd have worked it out. As it was, I kept my pride and said nothing, pretending I was just fine and could keep up.

Had Herb had been hiking with us in Cornwall, he no doubt would have stopped me. He learned self-protection when he was young, fleeing from Nazi Germany as a child, surviving an orphanage in London, crossing the Atlantic in a ship during wartime with his family, and he learned how to take care of himself. He was a survivor; he was my teacher.

I miss him every day, but I am grateful he does not have to witness the current versions of political madness—for the second time in his life. Our current politics would have broken his heart, I think, as he deeply believed in the America that saved them when they fled for their lives.

I wonder, does every generation have to go through the kind of hardships that make us so fearful? I cannot believe our species is incapable of mutual care and compassion, of intelligent creativity, of gratitude and love. We depend upon one another for life, after all, and we depend upon the health of the earth itself for our survival, but we are brought up to compete, to fight and win. In essence, we are brought up for war.

How crazy is that?

And still, I live with the struggle for self acceptance, even at my age, and the simple wish to love and be lovable—even when I make the mistake of bringing the wrong shoes.

Here on the farm we are trying to counter our society's pattern by living together and getting to know one another across lines of culture and color and belief system—not so easy during a lock-down! Each of us comes from people who have historically been harmed by poverty, racism or violence, and each of us, I would venture to say, suffers from some version of feeling inadequate amongst the others. Certainly, angry—and with reason.

We descend from Africans, native Americans, Middle Easterners, Asians, Europeans East and West, South and Central Americans—all lands that have been colonized by force. (Imagine the inherent shame for those who have been colonized..)

Our ancestors all arrived at some point in time to this continent, either brought against their will or fleeing for their lives from poverty or terror. Some came earlier, others came—or were forcibly brought—more recently; some have light skin and others rich brown, but none of our ancestors were exempt from suffering. Not one.

We are a melting pot of survivors who have been through exceptional horrors, separately and together, and we each have been informed by the experiences of our lives. As we heal ourselves of our traumas, I believe we heal one another, embracing our collective shames and terrors and rocking in one another's arms, weeping and singing until we can take big breaths of forgiveness and self forgiveness.

I believe we are amazing, every one of us! We have survived despite attempts to enslave us, erase us, humiliate us but we are still here, bruised and inflamed and outraged, but not broken!

We have nothing to be ashamed of, especially if we can laugh and cry, because we have been tested and tried. We have come through true.

Take a breath.

Take a bow.

Scary Times

for Alonzo King

Years ago I had one of those life-changing dreams that happen if we are very lucky, and it is as clear to me today as it was the morning I awoke from it:

I am high in the hayloft of a large barn, looking down, and below me is a circle of dancers brightly dressed, swaying and stamping to the beat and laughing as they do-si-do from one partner to another, weaving themselves into a gorgeous, colorful fabric as they dance.

I watch from high above them, but at the same time I am also right there on the barn floor with them, one of the dancers, hand in hand with my friends. My hips sashay sexily to the music, with my nose I breathe in the sweet musk of baled hay in the loft above us, my skin feels the tickle of sweat on my face and giggles rise up and out from my throat.

I dance from partner to partner, grasping one hand after another as my feet stamp to the beat of the music along with the others and see their colorful costumes pass before my eyes—orange, blue, red, purple. I grab a girl's hand, then a boy's, then the girl with black hair and then the fellow in the rainbow shirt until I twirl back to my own partner again, laughing and laughing until I am dizzy and out of breath.

But at the very same time I am watching quietly from above in the hayloft, mesmerized by the mandala of the *whole* design even though I am still dancing and laughing in the circle down below.

Both of the scenes are real. Above and below, they take place at the same moment in time, separate only because I am seeing them from different perspectives simultaneously—one being lived on the ground in the moment, and the other witnessed from above as a Whole design.

Like Life.

I find myself doing that a lot these days, watching the world through multiple lenses at once. I see the everyday realities of burning lands and rising oceans that put our lives in jeopardy every day, and the fear and mayhem that inevitably follows it. I watch the breakdown of societies as we know them; the terror of refugees fleeing war and hunger; the destruction of the natural world for profit.

At the same time I see the inevitable, ongoing cycling of Time over thousands of years in which whole societies and worlds eventually collapse, renew and emerge eventually into new eras, cycle by cycle. In Sanskrit, these are called *yugas*. Time Maps also exist amongst many ancient cultures—the Maya, the ancient Hindu, the African Dogon …

The world we know and live in may indeed be on its way out, to replicate a process that has happened before, and will happen again. I sometimes wonder if I was born in these times to witness this process of inevitable renewal; in fact—maybe that is what writing these pieces all these years has been about?

I keep being reminded of the pains of childbirth when my own children were born, and I wonder if what we are collectively going through on earth now is like labor pains on a larger scale?

With my first child, after nine months of carrying him around in my body, labor started with small stirrings of change as my belly tightened, then released … then tightened again. Gradually, as the rough beginnings of labor rumbled in, becoming harder and harder to ignore, I had to stop and breathe frequently, getting used to the increasing pains. Soon I had to lie down and breathe. Whew! It got harder and harder—hour after hour of hurting—and when the pains started coming in without let-up, Herb called the doctor and got me to the hospital in the middle of the night, racing through the high water and winds of a winter storm!

"Sorry for the timing," I gasped, trying for a joke when we got there at 2am. But it still took another few hours of continuing contractions, the pain increasing and waning … increasing and waning before this baby, blind and untested, fought his way through the narrow, dark tunnel inside me, my labor pressing upon him, squeezing his little body towards the light and air.

And then—the pain grew and grew until there was nothing to do except to PUSH! And just when I had no more energy to push with, he crowned—and my baby was born!

New life in the world.

Yes, in these days as we try to understand what is being born into this world, I am as terrified as anyone. I am also watching from the 'hayloft' high above and see a larger reality in which the dance is always changing, dissolving and evolving into more complex forms of color and shape and motion. I am a watcher and a dancer at the same time, sensing new patterns trying to emerge into this world of ours, recognizing that nobody ever said it would be easy!

Like childbirth.

I watch for the patterns every day in every way, intuitively feeling for a sense of wholeness in what may be inevitable processes we are going through. To me, it is all ultimately powered by Love, the highest frequency that encompasses everything in Time and Space that we call our *world*.

Hard though it may feel to us, I believe we have to trust it because—as with labor, there is no other way—except *through*. We have no choice but to keep breathing with it! That's just the way it is.

People like me have, through the Ages been called 'mystics'—and have also been shunned as witches and burned for their beliefs. *My* beliefs, as it happens.

Here is what I see, and what I believe to be true:

That the Earth we inhabit is only one point in a much larger universe, and that Life itself may be intrinsic to a cosmos in a multitude of forms, rising into material existence and then out again, through death, and back into Time and Space from its birthplace in pure consciousness.

That humanity on Earth is one life-form amongst many, and that consciousness itself is the template upon which whole worlds emerge and take meaning.

That awe is the appropriate response to the majesty of where we human beings—and all of life and the dimensions of the world that life inhabits—come from.

That, by definition, we humans are inextricably connected to one another, in balance, in beauty, in brilliance, and that murdering one another—by any means—is unworthy of our gift of life and our talent for delight.

And that we take our place amongst many millions of life forms on our planet, like a web of tiny pearls all connected by the string of life—remove one, and the whole string breaks.

And we are only *one* planet amongst many; one planet in a multitude of planets and solar systems in a Space that goes way beyond where our telescopes can currently reach, and ultimately, I believe, there is nothing to fear because we actually live in ALL of it!

I live by these truths and universal patterns in which we ultimately have our lives and beings. I believe in the sacred nature of a conscious Cosmos in which every atom contains the intelligent design of the Whole—even now when we humans are lost and frightened. I believe in a bigger picture that we can learn to decipher once we are ready to accept that it is there.

Please come and join me in the hayloft and watch with me. Then we'll go downstairs and join the dancers dancing their dance.

Dancing *our* dance!

Enormous Changes

*for Leon, in memoriam,
for Deb and for James*

Before midnight on New Years Eve, my younger brother left this life. A farmer in Vermont, he had been out clearing brush in the fields two days before and now was taking his regular afternoon nap before friends arrived for the evening. In the waning hours of both the day and the year he took his leave of us quietly without any fuss, as was his way.

In Deuteronomy it is written that such a death is "a kiss from God." It is not surprising that this dear man—farmer and scholar, musician and activist—received such a blessing as he took off to join the angels.

Now I am the only sibling left.

In a moment, just like that, all is changed. Left behind, I hover between the worlds, following him on his journey in my heart and mind as I also walk across the kitchen floor on my own two feet. I am not sure what is real right now, nor what is dream; I am afloat in more worlds than one.

A few weeks ago I had an odd, similar experience though—perhaps a precognition—in a Goodwill store where I'd gone to find a soup pot cover, and on my way out passed by the Ladies' Pants section where I stopped to pick up an extra pair of jeans. I found them, checked the tab for the size and saw my married name written on it, "Carolyn Strauss."

No … I took a slow breath and looked down at the tab again. My name was still there. (This was before Covid.) The store was there, people wandering the aisles, conversations, the quiet clack of hangers. I stood very still, feeling as if I were dreaming while awake, not quite knowing where I was. If my name was *still* there, I thought, I'd know for sure I was dreaming, so I looked down …

It was.

"I will try to pay for these, and then I'll know …" I thought, moving very slowly towards the check-out station. In the dream I paid four dollars. Would I find my car in the parking lot … ?

Step by step I followed the familiar routine of unlocking the car, getting in, starting the engine and driving home—very slowly. Only when I parked at home did I look down again at the tab.

My name was still there.

In the house, I fell into a fitful nap. When I awoke later, my name was still on the tab and my hands began to shake. Then I grabbed my computer and typed in my name—and discovered a rather chi-chi dress designer in New York City by the name of Carolyn Strauss!

For an hour I couldn't stop laughing, relieved but also wondering if this experience of hovering between realities might be significant for some reason. And it was, for I've learned what it feels like to be between the worlds, experiencing both at the same time and seeking a new kind of balance there. I had been in both waking and dream reality simultaneously, and recognized that *both* were real, which now helps me relax into an expanded sense of the world we live in.

And accept my brother's death.

I think it was a teaching for this time in the world, too.

Things are shifting before *all* our eyes in fact, as we clear last year's brush from our mental field of vision, as my brother was doing on the farm, and make preparations for what comes next.

I imagine he is there now in the multi-dimensional existence of Time and Space where all Being is woven into a rich fabric that contains not only what we know as our world, but also cycles of reality that include so much more than that.

What we call 'death' is, of course, an integral part of the process.

Most of us are terrified of dying, and our rational minds cannot comprehend it, but by the peaceful expression on Leon's face I'd guess there is nothing to fear.

Herb saw something ineffable too, as he was leaving, and in fact reported back while he still could that the "worlds and worlds" he saw were "profound and powerful!" His eyes actually shone with wonder.

"Oh, the big Love!" breathed my friend Jessica as she passed over, her face radiant. And my brother's face, in death, was relaxed and peaceful.

"Show us how?" I want to ask him. I can hear him chuckle, suggesting it is time we'd learned how, and quick, because things are changing very fast in the world now, and it's best we be able to move rapidly when it is time.

A few days ago a big earthquake hit Puerto Rico; and fires are sweeping across Australia. England and Scotland are under floodwaters and the ice is melting on the Poles. For those who live on this planet—human, plant and animal—it is time to act—NOW!

Resisting the inevitable is not an option.

"We didn't even have time to grab the family pictures!" cried my friends who fled from the Santa Rosa fires in the middle of the night. "Not even a stitch of clothing!"

They survived, but others did not.

So, given the reality of great changes in the offing, how do we prepare? In my heart, I am asking my brother for advice. "What should we be doing, Leon?" I see a slow grin starting on his face.

"Well, why don't you start by planting some sunflowers..?" he suggests. "That always helps. Then remember to sing ... music really can make a difference and, uh, love one another no matter what, no matter where, no matter how ..."

Or who?

I take a big breath, and the tears make waterfalls on my cheeks and run down my nose.

Then I hear him add, "Y'know, it only takes 144,000 people to tip this world from Big Fear to Big Love—really. Try that—every little bit helps. It doesn't take that many people to make a tipping point, you know."

I nod, but really, I didn't know.

"And," he continues while I sob, "uh, *please* don't forget the sunflowers ..."

Scared to Death

I grew up scared. My people were frightened refugees, and my boyfriend was a survivor of the Holocaust. Our lives were shaped by fear, as were our neighbors', so once I was old enough to leave, I went back to the Old Country to see where I came from. I was also keen to check out all those Medieval Churches with Hell scenes sculpted in stone, showing sinners being pitched into boiling oil by leering devils and hung upside down over Hellfire. I wanted to see for myself that Medieval campaign to scare the wits out of ordinary folks by showing them what happened to sinners who disobeyed the rules. As a habitual outsider to rules, I figured it was a good thing to know what I might be in for!

Anyhow, I had to get a handle on my own fears: of the dark; of bad dreams; of my maturing body and of the madness in my family. So I went off to "study Catholics" as my parents put it, who did not realize that I was actually going off to study myself.

Then came the day a light came on, and I got it that by studying Medieval Art History in France and learning about Christianity, I was also indirectly learning about the Judaism I was brought up with! And

I understood that the fear of Death was implicit in both religions, which seemed to be teaching by fear!

Oh!

I still shudder to recall those nights of despair in my little feath-erbed beneath the eaves where I was a nanny in Poitiers, trying to understand death itself, and how I could possibly not exist in this world. Was that what we all were scared of, more than pain, poverty or loneliness? More even than each other?

I eventually realized that my fear was of an unthinkable state of 'not-being' in which the 'me' thinking that thought did not even exist! Erased by Death, there was simply no more thinker—or me!

That was really scary!

Then I had this dream:

I am walking precariously at the edge of an ocean cliff, the sea stormy beneath me. One careless footstep and I could fall over to be dashed to death on the rocks. Carefully, I place one foot after the other —but then lose my footing, falling precipitously to my death below! But instead of landing on the rocks, I float! I am suspended easily between sea and sky, not dead at all, but no longer bound to the earth.

I am simply elsewhere …

I trusted this as a teaching dream; that we transform from our solid human bodies at death into transparent forms on a higher level of frequency—like a different station on a radio band—but our minds and memories and awareness remain quite intact.

So as we now ponder the global Coronovirus, the spectre of Death knocking stealthily on all our doors, I am touched by our various human responses, from being collectively terrified, to stocking up on toilet paper, to recognizing the collective nature of our species and indeed, all species. We are in this together, and even though we have been denying that fact for centuries, it is time to take it seriously, and act accordingly.

Why have we humans been sold a bill of goods about competition and war, with jealous Gods meting out punishments and parceling out the earth to colonizers who 'rule the waves?' Who made up that fairytale?

I have no idea, except we know that scared people are controllable people.

And we are good and scared now, so do be careful!

The reality is that everything in the world, from electrons to galaxies, and all of Life in between, have cycles. Cycling is a pattern of the natural world, so why not us as well? We call our cycles of coming in and out of physical form Birth and Death, but tend to ignore that consciousness, or the Spirit level of our Beings is a background constant within which all phenomena exist. So these bodies we wear for each human lifespan have a finite time in the world, but our consciousness, which belongs to the Universe itself, simply re-joins the Mother Ship and continues on.

I find that rather exciting, like packing up for an adventure on the other side of the world where we just may meet the love of our life! Every moment will be a new surprise, and every mountain we climb will present a whole new vista!

Don't get me wrong—I love this life, but when it is over, whenever it is my time, I expect I'll be as excited as I was on my first date with Herb, that tall guy with the soulful eyes who I eventually married.

So, what to do now as we move day by day into the realities of a pandemic? Do we freak out with fear, do we pay no attention, or do we figure there may be something important to learn from all this? And if so, what might that be?

I'd suggest we figure out how to use this dilemma intelligently, because it is way past time in the world to make some basic changes. We can do it, I know.

I received this yesterday, by the author Paul Levy, and it speaks to me, so I will share it with all of you.

"One of the major symptoms of the coronavirus is that it induces fear—which is known to weaken the immune system, thereby allowing the virus to more easily propagate itself. When fear is collectively mobilized, due to its psychically contagious nature, it takes on a seemingly autonomous and independent life of its own, feeding mass panic that easily turns into a collective psychosis. To see through the illusion of the separate self is at the same time to take away the power that fear has over us (as well as to empower ourselves), for the experience of separation and fear (of "the other") mutually co-arise, reciprocally reinforcing each other. Genuine compassion (which strengthens the immune system) is the result of this realization."

Yes.

Stay safe.

With love, Carolyn

Emergence or Emergency?

About 20 years ago, I met the Psychiatrist Dr. John Mack at a gathering to celebrate his new book, *Passport to the Cosmos*, which was about his work with people who had experienced what were called 'alien abductions,' and this week, I am finally reading it. I don't know why I waited so long to pick it up—perhaps because, soon after that evening, he was 'mysteriously' run over and killed by a drunken driver and his work had all but gone underground. The possible implications of his untimely death felt too awful to focus on at the time, but now I am ready. This book is affecting me deeply now, as the testimonies of these people who sought help from Dr. Mack all describe their experiences in essentially positive terms. It is what they learned in the process that resonates for me—and did for Dr. Mack, as well.

I wish I could meet them all now. They express feelings that resonate for me, experiences I share even though I have not gone through anything even vaguely like these 'abductions.' They speak of being shown how they merge with the whole Universe, body, mind and spirit. They experience what one woman calls the 'love glue' that holds everything in the world together. One speaks of her abduction experience as a "school to help her remember what she already knew about herself and all things being part of God." They are shown that death is nothing to fear, that we cycle in and out of material existence on the earth plane in the natural course of events.

Imagine … there is nothing to fear …

These days on Earth we are terrified as our environment breaks down under the mistakes caused by our culture's limited vision of the material world and the economics based upon it. We quail under wars and deprivation, pandemics and rising seas. Like masked bandits, we put distance between ourselves and our friends, and teach our children to be afraid. We're at a tipping point, no doubt about it, and it is goading us into making some essential changes in our ways of thinking about the world before it is too late. Can we do it? I believe we can, because, well, we must.

When I feel hopeless—and relatively *helpless,* as I do now—I remind myself of that broiling late summer day several years ago at a rain dance in New Mexico, when dancers and drummers beat out repeated rhythms under a relentless sun in the pueblo dancing grounds, hour after hour from early dawn to day's end. It looked a hopeless task if ever there was one, but also an ancient one that, I was assured, mostly always worked.

Heat and dust and the pounding of tireless feet, hour after hour until, just before sunset the clouds moved in as if from nowhere, the skies opened up and the storm came on, huge raindrops pelting down on us and turning the dust to mud in minutes. Water gushed through the pueblo and the dancers, one by one came to a halt, lined up quietly and got pelted by the rains they had magically called up by dancing non-stop together for a whole day.

Magic? Well, yes, but we live in a magical world, even when all evidence seems to point to the contrary. But there it was, cold rain on my skin and puddles at everyone's feet as the elders took their places on the roof of the Kiva and sat quietly together, getting soaked. The evidence was indisputable; whatever we happened to believe or not believe was not the point: a community dancing together all day long had brought the rain!

It is my memory of those young dancers being pelted by the rainstorm at the end of a scorching day of dancing and drumming in the desert that gives me hope now. In a purely material world, it makes no logical sense. Such a thing cannot happen. But in a world open to the unknown, where even 'magic' may be real—as it always has been for indigenous people—then anything is possible—even spaceships from other worlds. Who says we know everything there is to know? After all, it *did* happen.

Anyhow, if we can walk, we can dance; if we can talk, we can sing which means most every one of us has access to this magic. Whyever not let it in? Shakespeare says it in Hamlet:

> *There is more in Heaven and Earth, than there is in your philosophy, Horatio.*

Why turn down such a gift, and stay afraid?

I learned something profound that day in the desert sun, and it has informed my life ever since, so I dance and sing frequently to find that subtle balance point where "all is well, and all manner of things are well" no matter how horrendous the news. It helps; it really does.

I have also been at the bedsides of friends and family as they lay dying—especially during the early days of the AIDS epidemic—and I watched as they made their transitions. In almost every case, as they took their last breaths, their expressions shifted into something like wonderment, or joy.

"Big love!" whispered Jim, his eyes shining just before the end.

"Wow, oh wow!" mouthed Steve Jobs as he passed over.

My husband, a stalwart scientist all his life whispered to me in awe on his last day, his weakened arms tracing spirals in the air as he showed me the "worlds and worlds" he was seeing, his eyes like candles, "This is so profound, this is so powerful … "

Apparently, it is that larger picture that was revealed to those people "abducted by aliens" (our language, not theirs) and given a glimpse of the larger picture of a multi-dimensioned reality that encompasses our three-dimensional material world.

"I am an infinite being connected to all that is," said one person who consulted Dr. Mack after her abduction experience.

Said the ancient Chinese sage, Chuang Tzu, in 300 B.C.

> *Birth is not a beginning, death is not an end.*
> *There is existence without limit; there is continuity without starting point.*

Whyever would we not believe such testimonies?

Coping with Despair

for our children

Let me start by admitting that I am rather bad at coping with despair, my own or anyone else's. It's been a hard time lately, for multiple reasons, and I've felt lousy so I've been rolling out of bed early and driving down to the Bay for quiet times by the water while the fog slowly lifts off the dark clouds coming in from the ocean. I just sit there quietly, melting back into my dreams of the night, sometimes writing them down, sometimes not.

It used to be, in years gone by, that seabirds filled these morning skies—seagulls, cormorants, guillemots—and they are now almost gone. Migrating ducks used to fly in and cover the lagoon and the seals slipping in and out of the waves seem to be no more. Even the red-winged blackbirds! In my short lifetime, the wildlife here has all but disappeared.

My heart is heavy as I let myself doze off, sitting on this familiar bench in the growing light—a bench dedicated to a man I once knew—and I find myself begging him for some sign of reassurance that we will make it through, even though it doesn't look good. Please, John …

I fell asleep, hearing the lulling rhythms of water against the shore rocks and the occasional call of a seagull. And then something, like a signal to pay attention, opened my eyes and in the air above me six pelicans sailed across in a perfect V. I stared at the now-empty sky in a kind of thrall, and then came fourteen more (I counted them) in a gaggle of wings and flurries, as if catching up to reassure me that pelicans, at least, were still here, even after their species had apparently died out from the effects of DDT thinning the eggshells in their nests. For years they were gone from our skies, but we apparently had caught our mistake in time and here they were, back over the water, sleek and beautiful!

I believe the birds. And then also the seals—I haven't seen one in this Bay for years—but there was a seal who popped her sleek head out of the water just now and dove seamlessly under the waves right in front of me, as if to reassure me! I believe she was smiling.

Oh, thank you!

We had caught our mistake and healed it ...

We can do this, I know, because my own life—and no doubt each of our lives—is studded with mistakes and humiliations and unfair punishments that we have survived and hopefully learned from. Living in frightening times we are all under stress—'traumatized' is the word of the day—trying to do our best under the duress of injustices beyond naming—insane economics, racism and fear—trying to not get harmed in the melee while not hurting others—but our skins are thin, (mine is, at least) and our insecurities are like sore thumbs that keep getting banged by the same hammer.

Owww!

Then the old hurts get triggered and we feel helpless with despair. For myself, I dissolve in self-dislike, appalled by my ridiculous weaknesses.

Oh no, not again!

Even after all these years and so much self-examination, when I am taken by surprise by some new mortification, big or little, I am immediately taken back to my wedding day—one of the most humiliating days of my life—because my father, not for the first time, was out of control. Furious with me over something or other, without warning he grabbed my shoulder and slapped me hard across the face—in my pretty white wedding dress, with flowers in my hair, my brand new white shoes …

My mind went blank and I tried to run …

(This story is one I never wish to recall, but always do.) The point is that I barely remember how Herb got between us, covered me with his body and got me out of that room. I do remember sobbing out to him, in the hallway, that if he needed to annul our marriage, I understood; this was indeed my family, and he'd be totally justified in having second thoughts about marrying into us.

I meant it, too.

"You're my lawfully wedded wife," he whispered in my ear, tears in his eyes to match mine, and we retreated to the Coat Room to cry together before slipping out and starting what would be our marriage of 57 years, which turned out indeed to be an ongoing adventure—a damn good one, and pretty sane, all things considered.

My father died before his 50th birthday. May he rest in peace.

Breathe …

The marks are there, yes they are, and many wounds still unhealed but together we made a go of living well in a troubled world no matter the obstacles we had to climb over. No matter how hopeless it all looked—Herb was, after all, a childhood survivor of the Nazis—we learned how to walk through the fires of our time and treat each other well in the process.

And produce three fine new people.

Together all five of us, learning how to love.

Scared to death much of the time.

But together.

Together.

Gobsmacked

The other night I had a nightmare of being covered with oily beetles in clumps all over my body. I could feel them crawl down my legs and up my chest, their pointy feet prickling my skin and their hard bodies clicking as they rubbed against one another. I woke up gagging, still trying to scrape them off my skin.

It took two days before I realized that the bugs were my dreamlife symbol of the Corona virus, and the dream was telling me that viruses were part of life itself, and always have been. We could not live without them.

In my dream, the bugs crawled down my knees past my feet and into a hole in the ground, gradually becoming compost for the roots of plants. They belonged here and had their own job to do, even if they gave me the willies.

I think about this a lot as I watch myself and all the rest of us respond to this pandemic. I only keep half an eye on death statistics and fear-based politics, but choose to focus on the creativity of the young ones coming out all over the world: the collaborations of music and dance that bring tears and laughter and such deep gratitude to me; the thoughtful information given freely; the Zoom choirs and theatrical productions.

I also am grateful to the virus that is stimulating this brilliance!

Collectively, we are being pushed into more of our innate creativity than we thought we had, and the scope of our imagination under duress is blowing me away! We are in this together and many of us are determined to have a blast being the geniuses that we actually are.

Yay!!

Yes, of course there are very real victims to this pandemic, and I may well be one of them before this is over. I do not make light of the suffering and dying, but victims of our inhumane policies have always been suffering and dying, hidden in plain sight long before we ever heard of Covid-19. Five million children starve worldwide on a yearly basis; innocent victims of poverty, war, and racial injustice hang onto life everywhere. I see them right here in the Bay Area, where I live, camping at the edges of freeways and huddled on city sidewalks, begging.

Unnecessary poverty and death in our societies are not an anomaly; the difference may be that now we are paying attention.

Since the virus crosses political lines—it even crosses oceans—nobody is left out of the picture, not you, not me.

It is an Equal Opportunity bug.

I find it fascinating to watch our collective response to shared fear as we greet one another from a distance, reading the expressions in our eyes above our masks, looking for kindness and melting with gratitude when we recognize somebody we know. I sense we are learning fast how strong our need to know one another is, because we're all in this together, come what may. We may even be discovering how glad it makes us to feel needed, and how pleased we are to lend a hand!

An aside: I just learned that my friend Shadi has been bringing cat litter to her elderly friends—this is a woman who understands how essential a beloved pussycat is to someone living alone. I love this woman who knows how to see the bigger picture with generous humor!

I am gobsmacked (I love that word!) by how quickly we are responding to our shared threat with generosity! The feeling reminds me of the black-and-white film, *The Secret Garden*, I saw so many years ago, that moment when the children creep into the walled garden they have been secretly tending and the film bursts into full Technicolor! Climbing roses and apple blossoms buzz with ecstatic bees, purples and yellows and reds bloom out of the deep greens of leaves and grasses and velvety moss while the golden sun shines in a bright blue sky … I remember feeling ecstatic.

That is happening right now!

It is Spring here—though I learned today that it is snowing in Vermont—but here the caterpillars are swelling in their cocoons, fit to burst their skins and emerge as changed creatures and take to the air in flights of rare beauty.

Yesterday we had a rumble in our neighborhood—that is, infected by a similar impulse but not so graceful as the butterflies—ambulance sirens and honking police cars and roaring fire-engines stormed into our streets, blaring! I ran out of the house, as did many neighbors, looking for the perpetrators.

"I pray it's not someone killed a police officer," Kerry the mailman said, crossing his fingers, "We don't need that now …"

"Not to worry!" shouted Marjorie, "I just read it's a celebration to thank all the workers at the hospital!" We laughed together, waved to one another, and went back into quarantine.

Back inside I turned on YouTube and watched my musical hero Stejpan Hauser on his cello alone in the center of a huge Roman arena in his home town of Pula, in Croatia, surrounded onscreen by Zoom squares of workers on the front lines there, masked and doing their jobs on empty streets. I sobbed hard through the whole thing, grateful for the depth of my emotions. Then I watched a young tenor sing a Puccini aria in his pajamas—with changed lyrics, of course—and laughed until I was weak.

Laughter and tears … release.

We're just past the full moon and in the midst of a huge turning point that has been in cocoon phase for much of our lives. In this transitional time, the old and the new coexist for quite awhile as the balance tips and the Light comes into ascendancy. Even though the Negative forces are holding on with insane tenacity, time is on the side of the Positive. It is our task, I believe, is to be unafraid of the mystery of these world cycles and have the best time we know how to have!

Change happens, as the saying goes, and the Old Guard resists—of course, that's its job—but it is being eroded daily by our world-wide collaborations based on love and connectedness such as we have not seen before. I learned it has been estimated that those working to exemplify Love as a template for the world outnumber the current power elite by a million to one!

I believe it is our ability to take on this time with a sense of fun and wonder, being wildly creative with everything we can think of, that will raise the frequency of the whole planet and shift, shift, shift our consciousness out of its limited material grayness and into the Technicolor garden of humanity's next phase of existence.

What an amazing time to be alive in the world!

Do you suppose, maybe, we all wanted to be part of this celebration, and so chose to be here now … ?

Covid Quarantine

I am sometimes taken to task for sending out these 'positive' messages while there is so much evil happening in the world.

"Don't you see what's going on?" they demand.

Of course I see it—that's why I try to remind myself, and us, of the opposite. This seems to be my assignment these days: to help keep our spirits up while we do the difficult job of shifting our consciousness to a finer plane of being, a higher frequency of vibration. We are at the end of an era and transitioning into the next, and we have to find our way onto this new level without being destroyed by fear, as old patterns break up into chaos, making space for the new patterns that are still being created.

I believe these times are about profound change.

Nobody ever said it would be easy, but that doesn't mean we can't rise to the occasion, especially with the help of everyone and everything we can imagine—and also some we couldn't imagine, like Covid, for example.

Yes, it is terrifying. But it is also an amazing opportunity for us—all over the globe—to stop and take stock of where we are, who we are, and what can possibly be coming next. Things were way out of hand in the world even before the virus hit, but then the universe gave us this whopper to deal with, and did it to everyone in the world at once!

What a brilliant move!

Everyone has a story to tell of these past few months. Mine is that I had to pack up house and home by myself, in quarantine in a pandemic, and move to a new place still not quite finished! I assumed it would be an impossible job for any woman my age to do alone, but then I did it!

I wonder how many of us, under all that pressure, have been surprised by our own strength?

It was probably time for something big to shock us into action, because the environment and our self-respect have been going downhill steadily for a long time now. Personally, I've been expecting natural disasters like huge earthquakes and fires to wake us up, so I figure we've gotten off relatively easily with Covid, even with the inevitable loss of life.

The fact is that an estimated three million children we have never heard of, worldwide, die of starvation every year and one child dies of hunger every ten seconds without our even noticing it—long before we ever heard the word *Covid*.

Tragic deaths are not a new phenomenon.

Given that perspective, the virus and the worldwide quarantine seem a relatively gentle way to get our attention. Every single one of us, from babies to octogenarians, are having to slow down and rethink our priorities during an enforced time-out. Hopefully, we will use this time well and make some fresh choices about the preciousness of life on earth and of one another.

For me, alone and making my way, day after day, through every room and closet in the house, I've been doing a life review. Every book, every bowl had a story attached to it, and I am laughing and crying as one memory spins into another from all those years of a rich life.

Friends tell me their stories of digging deep into their childhoods, of grieving past wounds and remembering past loves. So many of us are looking back at our lives, feeling old feelings and getting to know ourselves in new ways because now we have lots of time to do so.

I bow to the bug.

Have you ever heard of the Chladni patterns with sand on vibrating plates? Look it up! Dr. Chladni experimented with sand and powders placed on a vibrating plate—like a drumhead—which he then 'played' with a violin bow. The pitch of the sound vibrated the plate to a particular frequency, setting the sand into motion which was chaotic at first, but then settled into a clear pattern which held its shape as long as that pitch was held. But when the tone was raised in pitch, the sand again went crazy until it formed into a different pattern, even more intricate and beautiful than the one before. And that continued up the scale—pattern followed by chaos followed by a more complex pattern …

In physics this is understood as a disintegration period that precedes a stage of higher integration, and may be how the physical universe evolves. (Doing the same thing with Lycopodium powder on the plate, and Mozart in the air, Dr. Chladni actually got the powder to dance!)

I believe we are in one of those dissolving states now, and have been for quite awhile. On the ground it feels like total disaster—and in ways it is—but more deeply, I suspect it is a phase of transition to a higher order of being that we have to find our way through.

It reminds me of my flute playing days performing with local chamber music groups, waiting in the wings shaking with stage fright every single time. I wished I were anywhere but there. I've heard that the great cellist Pablo Casals also suffered bad stage fright, and often wished he'd broken his arm the day before so he couldn't go on!

But then it was our turn and I'd take a deep breath, walk onstage with the others and forget to be nervous.

I remember a joke from my student days playing flute in New York, in which a famous conductor is being asked by a stranger on the street, "How do I get to Carnegie Hall?" to which his kind answer is, "Practice!"

That's what this quarantine may be about for many of us—practice! We have to get ready to perform in a new era whose time has almost come. It may be a good thing that we have this enforced sheltering-in-place to prepare for it, learning the fingerings and the phrasings, feeling how to listen for one another and studying the new score with deep attention.

And perhaps we are like caterpillars waiting in the cocoon, holding still as cells morph into wings and internal juices mysteriously transform into a butterfly.

Like you, I am sheltering in place, watching the world from a new perspective and paying close attention to everything I feel. We are waiting offstage together, preparing ourselves to play a new music in the world that every single one of us has been born to do, whether we know it or not.

Of course we're nervous; who wouldn't be? But I believe many of us, in the long run, are quite strong enough to pass the tests.

After all, diamonds go through an awful lot of pressure before they become gemstones, don't they?

Endings to Beginnings

One day this week my steam iron conked out after years of faithful service and after that, just before I was ready to dial in for a two-hour conference call, my telephone gave up the ghost. Then, in case that were not enough, the bathroom light went dark right in the middle of a shower.

Tomorrow the house next door starts coming down.

The message is clear. It is a time of endings, with no new beginnings in sight.

But last night I dreamed I was making music with a group of people by scrubbing vegetables on washboards, very hard and fast! (My instrument was a Napa cabbage.) Such glorious sounds, with love and laughter in the air—music sublime, rhythmic, juicy and totally alive, like no other music I'd ever heard before.

And then the next day at the farmers' market, at the cabbage stand, in fact, I ran into my favorite local singer, Juliana Graffagna. I go to hear her sing whenever she performs and I was happy to finally tell her how healing her music has been for me all these years. She beamed. She rarely hears that from people, she said, and she's always wanted to find a way to use her music for healing. So I invited her to my studio for a demonstration of my sound-healing work and a day later she came and we sang together.

It was as amazing an experience as I could have wished for—rich new, and tender. She was so moved, she cried.

Me too.

If these magical moments are still possible in a world with so many dire changes and endings in the news every day, can we count on miracles happening in time, or are we simply cooked? Should we accept the 6th extinction in our lifetimes or is there another way through?

I just learned, for example, that we've just about closed the ozone hole in the atmosphere we helped put there 15 years ago, by eliminating the CFCs in our refrigerators.

If the ozone hole is reversible, what else might be possible?

I've been watching a nest in the vine right outside the door here on the farm, with its 4 hatchlings squeezed in tight, almost, but not quite ready to fly. The outer edge, where Mom perches to feed them, is tattered to strings, making them push together tighter against the other wall so they don't fall out. I get the impression she's ready for them to leave already. They're not so sure about that. When I peer in to check on them, their tiny black eyes peer back at me, scared silly.

They are *so* adorable!

I wonder how adorable *we* are to whatever entities are watching us do the same thing—hanging on for dear life to old ways that no longer fit us? If it were *me* watching, I'd find it more maddening than endearing, believe you me!

For example, we're all seeing one institution after another shut their doors for not being financially profitable: hospitals have to close because they cannot afford to stay open; orchestras are disbanding because they cannot pay their musicians a living wage; students are in debt to Financial Aid companies and families cannot pay the rising rents or mortgages for their homes. Even my old high school has shut down!

And with each shutdown, people lose their livelihoods.

Piece by piece our culture's nest is crumbling out from under us, so we squeeze in tighter and pray we won't be the ones to fall off the edge.

This is either a totally insane system, or an extremely cunning one. As with the hatchlings in their nest, Mother Nature may be wisely doing Her thing, which is to push them/us out to make them do what they eventually have to do. They've got to gather up their courage, balance at the tattered edge of the nest, spread their untested wings and take to the air!

I expect it works because if you look up, trees and sky are full of birds on the wing!

If the birds can do it, we can too. All around the world people are starting to take things into their own hands, challenging the system and redefining how to live together, feed ourselves, teach our children, heal our sick. Food can be grown locally; people can share housing; children can be taught according to their unique talents; and land can be held in Public Trusts rather than as the 'private property' of a 'landlord' who has signed a deed that make him/her a Lord of *their* Land.

Up at the farm, in an area where housing costs have skyrocketed and many are leaving because they cannot survive here, a few intrepid souls are trying to provide another option: the Community Land Trust. The idea is that the land is put into a non-profit Commons, is cared for by succeeding generations who make their homes upon it, and the housing is affordable in perpetuity.

No speculation by developers is permitted; no single ownership; no banks involved; no profit to make. Hopefully—ever!

Since the very notion that a piece of the Earth can be owned by a single person or family whose lifetimes are measured in decades is patently absurd, there is no reason to keep such a rule. Nor to base a whole system of values and economy and institutions upon a notion as ill-advised and presumptuous as 'private property.'

It's as obvious as not selling guns to deranged people; nor tossing out surplus food when people are hungry; nor selling off our environment to the highest bidder.

I believe it's as obvious as knowing that birds have to fly when it is time because it's written into their DNA, just as making a change when necessary is written into ours.

I know there is magic, I know there are untrodden pathways we will walk, new music we will make, as-yet untested synapses in our DNA.

In these scary and exciting times I keep asking myself,

"What is my role in this process?"

What is yours?

Next morning: the baby birds have fledged!

My Vote

*for Noe and Bob and Christina and Massey
and the whole crew on Hilltop*

I go numb worrying over who to vote for—or even if I should vote at all, Lord help me!

For me, the real problem in the first place is the two-party system itself, as if we were playing some kind of Olympic Game—one winner takes the Gold Medal and everyone else goes home crying. What about the person coming in sixteenth place? I want to shout. Wasn't she also fabulous in her own way—even if she slipped on the final slalom?

My vote would be to rethink our Party system altogether, and maybe even replace it with something more interesting—and useful—like a lively collaboration amongst all the contenders, recognizing that each one has something unique to bring to the table.

Isn't it time for us humans to let go of the immature war model and grow up into adults?

I remember the elections we had for Student Council in high school, where we learned about government in the grownup world by 'running for office' with posters and speeches that promised great things if we were elected. As it happened, running just for the fun of it, I got elected one year, totally astounded by unexpected applause when my name was called. I was now Financial Secretary of PS 215—this girl who was all but flunking Math.

Even then, it was clear to me that the system was nothing but a popularity contest and had nothing to do with our abilities to do a job. I have thought of that over the years, election after election voting in the poll booth up at the Library, almost always walking away depressed for having to vote for the least objectionable of the candidates, not someone I wholeheartedly endorsed. Each time, I go home and eat chocolate ice cream until I feel better.

But at the time, Student Council meetings got me out of Math class every Thursday, so I didn't complain—but I've not been able to take our Party Politics system seriously ever since.

This time around, however, I just may listen to my deeper instincts and not go to the polling place, but start conversations with whoever feels a similar uneasiness. I figure that at my age it may be a now-or-never matter to take a stand, for we don't have time for monkey business! Damn it, the permafrost is melting and the oceans are rising—right?

But here we are still anxiously competing with 'the other side' when in reality *there is no other side!* We're in this together, like it or not. You'd think the Democrats, at least, would realize this and not fight amongst themselves! What are they thinking? Didn't they all used to be colleagues?

Breathe …

So what should we do? I take my cues, these days, from my late brother, who skillfully baked bread for the Draft Board and got out of the killing fields of Vietnam. And then went on to find land and grow food for his community. *That* makes sense to me.

"What would Leon do at this election?" I ask myself, and can see his whimsical smile as he shows me his latest repairs on the maple-sugaring shed—you see, it sags each winter under snow-loads, and he shores it up anew each spring with jigsaw-puzzle pieces of wood that create cunning abstract designs.

"Just look at it sideways to see the art," he'd suggest with a grin.

So, I've been dreaming up far-out projects to keep myself busy these days, pushing away some old assumptions about what is, and what is not possible, and going for broke.

If not now, then when, and if not me, then who? is my mantra.

So at the Wild and Radish farm there is an abandoned ranch house we've taken on to completely retrofit from floor to roof and everything in between. We want to demonstrate how an old, boarded-up wreck can be brought back to life as a 'Living Building,' with all materials and processes non-toxic and 'natural.'

The hope is to make a model of a living building that might help recreate whole boarded-up neighborhoods in our 'inner cities.'

So we design ways to sequester carbon, to copy the processes of water, energy, and waste the way Nature does it and bring all natural materials to the site from as close by as we can find them. And, since this is California, to make sure the house is as fireproof as possible.

It has been an exhilarating, long and totally filthy project as we demolish walls and toss out the old gas appliances, rotting foundations and fiberglass insulation. We're replacing ancient plumbing with pipes that carry graywater out to the gardens, laying old-fashioned linoleum in the kitchen, and exchanging the old insulation in walls and attic by wrapping the whole house on the outside with strawbales plastered with mud.

We're almost finished, and it's gorgeous! Imagine a house plastered with sub-stratum golden earth from a deep hole in the backyard! And imagine three gorgeous young women, splattered from head to toe with golden mud, doing the plastering!

There's a fair amount of grunting, but lots of laughter, and I notice that everyone seems to get along even when the going gets tough— which it does, of course, especially for those crawling on their bellies beneath the floorboards, masks over their faces to avoid generations of rat poop down there!

My take-away from this lively metaphor is that it's time for tearing down many old 'structures' that no longer serve us, and dreaming up new ways to live.

It is 2020, after all, and I'm told that this is the beginning of the new times in which we demolish old modalities and take our cues from how Nature does it, to create the new.

Which means we've got to be ready for some heavy demolitions, like it or not, including our two-party system but, I wager, starting with ourselves.

Well, starting with myself, at least.

For I take this mandate personally because it takes so much courage to acknowledge those stuck doors in myself, those old habits of thought and action I hold onto like a tiger, whether they serve me or not! But right behind my resistance, I can feel, more and more, the pressure of the love longing to burst through and come out, finally.

I'm tired of fear and stubborn egos, especially my own!

For those stuck doors are holding back tears of grief still waiting to be shed, and it will take a strong act of will to let them flow—I know, because I've tried. I expect a deluge, and it will come, no doubt. The metaphoric flood and the global one—both have happened before.

But right now my hand rises tentatively in greeting as my eyes search you out so we can cry—and then laugh—together.

What a relief!

Thank you for being so patient with me.

Virus: a Definition

I looked up the word 'virus' in the dictionary this morning, and got variations of this definition: "submicroscopic infectious agents that cannot replicate on their own but need a host cell in order to survive."

In other words, "We don't really know."

Unlike a bacterium, a virus is invisible even under strong magnification, so what exactly is it and where does it come from?

Again, we don't know.

As I ponder this invisible 'no-thing' that has us in its thrall, I am reminded of a day on the southern Brittany coast when I learned the hard way to pay attention to the larger contexts of things. I had walked out across the mud flats at low tide to a small island of seagrass about a quarter mile from shore to spend some quiet time writing. A few other people were there for picnics, and I found a small hollow to curl up in with my notepad.

I must have fallen asleep in the sun, and was awakened later by the sound of waves lapping by my side and realized I was alone on the island, the tide had come in and I was surrounded by open water.

Panic! In my wish for a perfect place to write, I had neglected to notice the larger context of this place—its regular tides, the time, the current phase of the moon, the history of the Morbihan coast. If only I had stopped for a moment to think! But in fact, all I took into consideration was my immediate desire for a pretty place to write.

Wading in ocean up to my armpits with my backpack held high above my head, I made my way back to shore amid laughter and congratulations of strangers who had watched the whole charade from the shore. I was even treated to a beer for providing such amusement to the locals!

We humans do that sort of thing—we get a great idea but neglect to think through the consequences, and then get stuck in a big mistake that can get us—or the earth itself—into a pack of trouble.

Scientists are as guilty of this as any of us, creating plastics that end up in landfills because nobody wondered what might happen after they were used, or splitting the atom to make a bomb! Maybe we're a little too smart for our own good—though not too wise—and maybe this pandemic will force us to stop for a moment and wonder how to live safely and well with one another on this planet.

As I write to you on my trusty computer, to which I am as attached as anyone, and prepare to send out this missive to friends everywhere, I learn from a talk by Dr. Thomas Cowan that the very technology that makes it possible to send messages across the earth in seconds may be at least partly what is causing this pandemic in the first place.

He asks a pretend question about dolphins who become sick after an oil spill has invaded their waters. "Would you examine the dolphins for pathogens to determine what is wrong?" he asks, "or would you presume the recently poisoned waters were probably what was affecting their well being?"

You know the answer. Dr. Cowan explains that a virus is not a 'thing' in itself, so much as an excretion of toxicity from a cell, and occurs when a cell is invaded by debris it needs to clean out. The poor so-called 'virus' itself is not the cause of anything! The cell is simply trying to purify itself by excreting whatever poisons are sticking to it!

All animals do a form of that as well; we call it, amongst other things, 'poop,' and consider it a healthy thing to do.

Puts a different spin on our dilemma, doesn't it?

So our cells, which make up our organs and our bones, our blood and our nervous systems, are what bodies that need clean air and water and healthy food in order to thrive, are made of, right?

But if we live in a polluted environment, our cells may be over-worked clearing out more toxicity than they were designed for, resulting in the so-called 'viral' loads that take us down. Adding noise pollution to that, and night skies alight with city lights to that, no wonder our cells are working overtime to get rid of more debris than they can handle.

Dr. Cowan also points out that we humans are electrical beings and that the ever-increasing electrification of our global atmosphere with new technologies beaming high frequencies from satellites high above our heads are of course affecting our bodies.

Given all of this, of course we're in trouble! Of course our cells can-not keep up with so much toxicity, and perhaps Sheltering in Place is a blessing in disguise.

As I watch myself slow down my pace, hang out in the garden to read, think and exchange news with my neighbors—six feet apart, to be sure—and go deeper into my thoughts and questions, sensory memories come up, along with gratitudes and longings, I find this break a Godsend. I am talking to neighbors who never had time before; I am cleaning closets untouched for years; looking through photos of yesteryear and reading favorite books again.

I love that people are again talking about Universal Health Care and that the canals in Venice are now clean enough for dolphins to swim in, and that people are singing together from their balconies—as I also sang in Ravenna all those many years ago when I was young and madly in love. I'm so happy to clearly hear, for the first time in memory, a Hermit Thrush singing for a mate in the garden and see, across the Bay, the clear profile of Mt. Tamalpais without its usual haze. From my bedroom window, I can even smell the new mugwort and lemon verbena plants down in the garden.

As we shelter quietly back into our own lives, it's as if we are able to recapture something of our birthright innocence—but with the advantage of age and experience. I've been waiting for an eventual breakdown of our society, and even preparing for it for a long time now. I've hoped it would happen while I was still here and strong enough to experience it whole, for I believe it is a shared initiation into the next phase of becoming.

We're all in this together, for better or for worse, even those in power who we love to hate. Personally, I'm finding that I love them all now—*US* all, even *him*—because we are all together in an existence much bigger, more interconnected, more Whole, than we might ever have imagined before this virus showed up!

I've learned, for myself, that it often takes some big bad trouble before I wake up and come to remember that I am living in the midst of a miracle, an enveloping, ever-expanding miracle of life with its ingenious mechanisms for maintaining itself in essential innocence against many odds.

Which is not the same as our childhood *innocence*, but different because coming *back* to innocence is an act of maturity and strength, being deliberately playful and ready to cooperate with grownup intelligence in the largest context we can imagine.

It's kind of like patting your head and rubbing your tummy at the same time—and laughing while you do it.

It takes some practice, but what else were you planning to do with your free time?

Changing the Pattern

Moving house and home after so many years has been a big deal made even bigger by 'shelter in place' rules, since being helped by family and friends has had to be scrapped. The work has been mine to do alone, which has meant clearing a three-bedroom family home of 50 years down to what could fit in the space of a retrofitted garage, and giving away all the rest. This at a time when thrift stores are in lock-down as well, and every object in the house is potentially contaminated—by myself.

Everyone I know—and many I do not know—have received gifts from me; even the house itself has been donated to a non-profit organization to provide affordable housing for local artists.

Doing all this has taken months of work, but I've mostly enjoyed it—recalling my life object by object and memory by memory, laughing and crying and giving away gifts. I've spent a lot of time on the phone, laughing with family and friends over shared memories, and deciding who would get what.

It's been a huge job, but it has mostly all gotten done, and I am now installed in my adorable retrofitted 'garage' surrounded by familiar rocking chairs and quilts, with good folks nearby and sheep and goats in the paddock right outside my windows, and I am living a brand new life—though still in lock-down—elsewhere.

Naturally, I have to make all the adjustments and shifts of mind and heart that accompany such a big change, and yes, it is a tall order, but I figure that changing the way we live is something we will all have to do sooner rather than later.

We are being stopped in our tracks by a tricky little virus or, as some say, being deluded into believing we are, or pushed by a madman to react to his madness, but the signal for big change is clear.

According to many ancient traditions, this time in the world is a time of breakdown, making way for new beginnings. We have little choice but to pay attention and make the required shifts in our thinking and behavior if we are to survive this era of change—as I discovered in my own life, having to jettison so much of my 'stuff' in order to move into my 'new life!'

Meanwhile, I've been reading *Shoes Outside the Door*, a book I rediscovered while emptying out the bookshelves. The book is an expose of an American-led Spiritual Center in San Francisco that came out over 20 years ago. I was a student there in the 1970s, and the author tells the story of the blatant misuse of power that happened around then, and the passive assent of students to obey rules clearly not in their own interest.

It is a human story and a story of our time. I lived through it, got out of there at a run when I understood what was happening, and learned some hard lessons in the process. I watched good folks obeying bad leadership without questioning it, making themselves as responsible as the perpetrators. Big, hard lesson!

If you were around at that time, you may recall the newspaper stories of a meditation hall burning down one night. It was big news, and the cause of the fire has forever remained a mystery! The author barely mentions it, probably because nobody he interviewed had a clue how it started.

I might, though.

As it happened, I was there that day but have never told anyone my version of the story, partly because nobody asked. I will tell it here, though, because it may be relevant to what we are experiencing now on a larger scale in the world.

It is about wrong uses of power and inappropriate obedience to that power.

I was, at the time, an independent student living with my husband and children away from the practicing community. There was a photographer, Nemo, who also lived outside the community, with whom I was collaborating on a book about the re-emergence of a burned-out forest in the mountains surrounding the monastery. About once a month, he and I would take off from the city well before dawn and arrive at the burn site with tripods and cameras.

In the growing light we'd slog through ankle-deep ash to find new green growing up through the old burn, and we'd set up the tripod, keep an eye on the rising sun, and start shooting. We got utterly filthy, and had the best times!

Visit by visit, the green forms became more evident as life spread across the blackened earth. I took copious notes and Nemo took pictures, showing me what he saw with his 'artist's' eye. I believe it was Nemo who taught me how to 'see.'

By the time the sun rose over the hill, we would pack up tripods and cameras and walk down to the monastery at the end of the road to wash up, chat with friends and have some breakfast before heading back to the city.

On this particular morning, we happened on a ceremony in progress, and stood by as a solemn procession of students robed in black, led by the head priest, emerged from the Hall.

We had no choice but to stand by respectfully, covered in soot and cameras as we were, and try to be inconspicuous—impossible by definition. I was shocked to hear the teacher hiss as he passed by us,

"What the Hell are you doing here? Oh, it's the novelist and the photographer ..."

Shocked, I tried to explain that we'd had no idea there was a ceremony going on. He ignored me and glared at Nemo.

This was my teacher?

Nemo, a gentle guy from Brooklyn who had grown up tough, growled a smart-ass comment about staying for breakfast, and from there it escalated into a contest of smears. The students kept their heads bowed, while the priest in silken robes and the well-known photographer in sweaty jeans exchanged insults.

"Unclear on the concept!" I wanted to scream. "Stop this!" But it escalated, so I moved in closer and yelled. "Cut it out, you guys!"

"We've been doing this for years," the priest laughed. I noticed that Nemo kept a straight face and the students mostly kept their heads bowed. Neither I nor the birds in the trees believed the teacher for a minute, and brushing himself off and bowing ceremoniously, he continued up the path followed by his obedient students.

I might have been invisible.

"What was that all about?" I asked Nemo once we put down our gear and took a rest under a tree.

"Oh, nothing much," he muttered. "We go way back. You hungry?"

"We haven't been invited," I reminded him.

"Oh yes ... yes we have!" he snorted, dragging me with him towards the Dining Hall.

Later, I ran back to the tree to be alone, but Nemo soon found me, and then the priest found him, and then the students drifted in to follow their teacher. It didn't take long before the two men were at it again, eyeing each other like prizefighters as they moved into a clinch, one in silken robes, the other in a sweaty tee-shirt.

"You fuckin' phony!" Nemo grunted, landing a hard punch at the priest, who countered with, "Scared I'll make you sit all night again?" Pow! Then Nemo, "Got married to prove you weren't gay?"

The insults were cutting closer to the bone and the students just stood around like jackasses!

We were in a monastery, for God's sake!

"Stop that!" I hollered, inserting myself rather dangerously between them and pushing with all my might to separate them before they drew blood. They finally gave way, panting and laughing unconvincingly.

I was certainly not convinced and neither were the birds.

"Sit down!" I ordered, as if I were in the playground with a bunch of eight year-olds. By this time more students had gathered—fascinated by the show, no doubt—and we were surrounded, but nobody moved forward to help.

The priest changed from dark to light, and laughing with a warmth that did not quite reach his eyes, called Nemo "Old buddy …" told whoever was listening that they had been fighting like this for years, and then removed a bracelet of skull-beads from his wrist and sat down on the log bench. The students hovered around, still silent as the priest chatted about this and that, and casually handed me the beads, otherwise still barely acknowledging my existence.

"What're those?" Nemo asked. We then were told a tall tale about shrunken skulls from an island off the coast of Ireland, and Nemo was again on his feet in fighting posture. The Priest coldly skirted around him and, totally ignoring me, strode by me, casually dropping the skull beads into my lap on his way.

"Oh, no you don't, mister," I muttered, taking off to follow after him, the skull bracelet in hand. "You forgot something," I called out to him as he approached the back door of the Hall. Without looking at me he turned swiftly, snatched the skulls roughly out of my hand and disappeared through the door.

It was over. All my commitment to the practice and the teachings and this man and this community, *gone* in one morning. I just wanted to get out of there and never come back.

This teacher badly needed a teacher! But that was not the end of the story:

That night the Hall mysteriously burned down during a night-time ceremony! Nobody has yet been able to determine how it started, but, we learned the next day, everyone got out safely, including the Teacher.

"They don't know what we-e know!" sang Nemo on the phone to me the next morning. Not only had the Hall burned to the ground—down to ash—but it also toppled a priceless ancient sculpture on the altar, breaking it into three pieces!

That all happened several decades ago. I, naturally, left the community shortly thereafter, the Priest has long since been deposed and after awhile the community finally rebelled. Meanwhile, huge debts incurred by reckless spending were either forgiven or paid off, and everybody hopefully learned some important lessons by the troubles. For me, watching the downfall of a brilliant, but troubled man was a painful lesson to witness.

The fact was that I identified with him; I even loved him; was grateful to him for teaching me some essential negative lessons as I watched him fall deeper and deeper into self-deception.

At my best, I have looked at my own self-deceptions and learned compassion for him and for myself. I finally recognized that we are all in this life together, for better or for worse. We each are students doing the work of liberation, taking a good hard look at our deep fears and longings before we can presume to teach others.

So here we all are, in global lock-down, with a precious opportunity to slow down and reckon with our own shadows, pulling out the weeds rooted in our tender and frightened hearts.

As the cosmos is a Whole, interconnected system of infinite proportions, then every single part of it is important and relevant, because nothing is outside the system. Nothing.

Not the Butcher, the Baker nor the Candlestick Maker.

Not you. Not me.

Red Clover

for Leon and Deb

It's the last harvest of the summer at Red Clover, the farm in south-eastern Vermont where my brother Leon lives with his partner Deb, and I've just spent the morning shelling beans. We've been out in the fields every day gathering in the corn and tomatoes, carrots and beets, peppers and melons and raspberries and squashes, storing them in baskets all over the kitchen; today we'll harvest the vines and make grape juice, and perhaps jar up more tomato sauce for winter. The last of the raspberries will get cooked up for tonight's dessert. Bit by bit all this produce will be dried or canned or frozen to get the folks through the long winter here.

I'm being a happy helper.

"Blood o' the earth," Deb says, holding up a bunch of fat red beets just pulled from the earth. I sniff and sniff until my whole body has memorized the smell of beets and earth and summer in this pristine part of Vermont, on this farm I've loved for 30 years with its views of the Connecticut River Valley, surrounded by dense woods of pine, beech and birch. And these dearest of people who have lived by their own rules since the 60s—hippies who grew up to become self-sufficient homesteaders.

For years I've admired this renegade younger brother of mine who escaped the choking confines of our household and made his way from being a confused kid in the suburbs to being a totally independent model of the new generation creatively changing how to live in a crazy world. Unlike many hippies of the 60s who dropped out only to drop in again, he stayed out.

It all started at his Draft Board interview during the Vietnam War.

Saying nothing to any of us, he showed up for the interview with a loaf of oatmeal bread he had just baked, a stick of sweet butter, a bread knife, a butter knife and a cutting board. Standing before the Draft Board and being the uncompromising idealist that he was, he told them he would not kill, no matter what.

"Even if someone raped your sister?" he was challenged.

"I simply don't know," was his honest answer. "But my real reasons are baked into my bread," he told them quietly, cutting the bread, buttering and handing each member of the Draft Board a slice.

I imagine they were bemused by this loony fellow or, as he points out, were just hungry since his interview was the last one before lunchtime. Maybe they assumed he was a hippie on drugs, or simply crazy, but the short story of a very much longer story is that Leon got out of the Draft with a classification nobody has ever heard of and was free to continue living his life with no official interference.

So while others were at an insane war on the other side of the world, my brother quit college in mid-semester and took to the road hitchhiking with his backpack and guitar. Eventually, he found himself in the quiet woods of Vermont where he pitched his tent by a ramshackle old farmhouse on 80 acres of meadow and woodland, learned how to live with others who had also escaped to the country, grow food in the summers and spend the long, cold winters delving into ancient Egyptian geometry.

And stayed.

Eventually, with the help of family and friends, these folks bought those 80 acres outright, Leon and Deb staying on to farm the land as country folk—pretty sophisticated country folk, I might add—while the others, one by one, moved on to careers and lives elsewhere after the war, becoming lawyers and artists and social workers—even one Oscar-winning actress—raising their children in the cities, but coming up to the farm for long weekends and summers.

Some, by now have died or drifted away, but most of the original group and their offspring—now into the third generation—remain a clan and continue to gather at Red Clover for weddings and Thanks-givings, work parties and memorials.

Over the years, I have gotten to know most of them.

Harvest time is "putting-by" time, and yesterday Deb and I put up tomato sauce and juice, cranking out tubs of it on a hand-grinder and bottling it up in one-gallon jars while Leon was out on the orange tractor, preparing beds for the winter-rye cover crop.

Deb and I danced to Salsa music as we peeled and squeezed squishy parboiled tomatoes through the hand-grinder, getting into the rhythm of plop, crank, and pour to a Cuban beat. By the time we were done and covered all over by tomato splatters, we and the kitchen were a lovely mottled shade of pink.

Then we ran up to the pond on the hillside and jumped in.

The clan gathered last week for the long weekend—all of us grey heads now—and we hung around talking with coffee cups as the morning sun warmed the meadows fragrant with new-mown grass, watched dragonflies skim the surface of the pond in the afternoons and later gathered at the fire pit for nostalgic suppers of barbequed chicken, beet salad and fresh-picked corn—catching up with each other, sharing stories, gossiping. One offspring had had a book man-uscript accepted by a New York publisher; another was building a studio; a new grand-baby had just been born.

A cell phone rang as we sat by the fire under the stars and with the magic of a technology that did not exist when these folks first stumbled here as young adults fleeing an insane world, there was the new baby on Skype! A beauty, we all agreed, singing his praises and congratulations to his parents on the screen and his grandparents right here by the fire.

How quickly the years had passed!

As the night wore on and the fire burned low, the conversation turned inevitably to the coming elections, the climate crisis, Alzheimers, dementia. Someone mentioned a new drug cure for depression and the discussion heated up: new therapies; other drug combinations; what they were trying out in Sweden …

I fidgeted, wishing I could argue for optimistic creativity rather than drugs, but I kept my own counsel. My brother, I noticed, was silent throughout the discussion, but listening. I caught his eye and saw the crooked grin start on his face as at last, in his own low-key way, he said,

"They could try growing sunflowers."

My hero. My bro.

Demolition

The old house next to the Wild and Radish farm had been boarded up for decades, sitting sad by the side of the main road until we bought it up this year. Right now it is down to rubble and its old wood framing, as we demolish the house layer by layer to rebuild it for its next incarnation. Our idea is to demonstrate how an old, worn-out urban building can be retrofitted with inventive technologies that support renewable systems and natural materials—and to make it beautiful! The whole process is being documented to demonstrate how this can be done, and the design plans will be made available to the public for the asking.

Bang! Bang! Out go rotting floorboards and crumbling plasters. Single-paned windows and gas wall heaters get tossed onto scrap heaps out in front, along with rusted pipes and filthy insulation. Our faces are masked against great clouds of ancient dust as we tear away at structures that no longer make sense, to replace them with technologies that take into consideration what the environment gives us freely—like straw and clay and sunshine.

At this point the house is nothing but a big mess, but it is very exciting to see light pouring through gaping window frames, and the space opening up from small, dark cubbies into gracious rooms.

We are a merry and innovative crew, rather pleased with ourselves as we hatch plans to insulate the house with an outside wrap of mud-plastered straw bales, and plumb pipes to take gray water out into the garden, while capturing the energy of sunlight on the roof and turning our food scraps into compost.

Taking on a green urban retrofit is something I've dreamed of doing for years, ever since riding the train from Vermont to New Jersey one summer and rumbling through one abandoned inner-city after another, seeing boarded-up tenements covered in graffiti and homeless people in makeshift tents on the refuse-strewn streets.

The memory still gives me a stomach ache and I feel relief that I can finally, with the amazing folks at Wild and Radish, start demonstrating, straight on, that it doesn't have to be that way.

It reminds me of a conversation I had long ago with an older woman when I was young and pregnant, about the pains of childbirth. I couldn't quite imagine how a baby could emerge from such a small opening! Ruth smiled her warm, knowing smile, touched my arm lightly and told me it would hurt like hell, but would be worth it in the end.

"The minute you hold him in your arms, you'll forget all about the pain," she told me. "Anyhow, the best things in life are always making some kind of a mess, right? Like sex or eating lobster—same with childbirth. But we're built for it."

Years later when she lay dying from cancer and I went over to say good-bye, she gave me her wan, knowing smile. "It's okay to be dying," she whispered. "Life's over, but what a chance to see what comes next…"

She held my hand while I cried.

I thought of her at the farm the other day, showing the sheep and goats to two little girls and their Mom. The small herd came to greet us *beh beh beh,* and we followed them, finding the old Grandmother sheep lying on her side by the fence, dead.

We must have gotten there shortly after her death because the younger sheep still surrounded her, nudging and staring, slowly going back to browsing on the hillside with our arrival, and gazing over at us periodically. Meanwhile, just across the way the demolition crew were banging and sawing away on the house unawares, tossing out the old to make way for the new.

Grandma-sheep Cocoa, in her life, had given us three daughters, milk for cheese and masses of springy dark wool for spinning, but now her time had come and we had to say goodbye.

It's the law of the world.

It seems everything is designed to do that: to cycle back into the elements after its allotted time on earth. There is birth, there is life, there is dissolution and there is death. This happens not only to plants and animals and humans, but also to houses, to cities, to civilizations, to planets … It could happen to us on Earth and indeed will, sooner or later.

I've been contemplating this probability as I age, and have been slowing down into my own dissolution phase, spending more time alone and in quiet. My thoughts want to deepen, my wonderments to open up, spanning longer tracts of our history and possible worlds beyond our star system. I read mythologies of the Maya, the Egyptians, the Hopi, comparing their parallel stories of great floods—more than just one!—and of their people's original homelands before the floods, places long since sunk out of sight and mind.

We may have been around on this planet way longer than we thought!

I read about earth changes that wiped out whole advanced civilizations in eras long before this one, of human skeletons unearthed with elongated heads and giant limbs—like us, but not like us; of lost technologies and ancient life-forms fossilized in oceanic mud; of seashell fossils high in the Himalayas and of unheard-of cities buried in the mid-ocean deeps.

Impossible! we might say, but who knows what impossible possibilities might actually exist?

I've experienced my share of these—though often unwilling to even mention them or be thought a fool—like the time Herb and I were in Chaco Canyon in mid-winter, and went invisible to one another in the ruins of Mesa Alta for two totally terrifying hours; or like arriving in the English countryside to visit a friend, when a crop circle pictogram, the length of several football fields, appeared overnight at a neighboring farm; or like the day I got messages from megalithic stones on the Brittany coast of France.

The stones 'spoke' to me that day on the hill above Carnac, I remember, where I was sitting atop an ancient dolmen in quiet contemplation. I had been on the Morbihan coast amongst the giant megaliths for some weeks and was saying farewell to my favorite places before taking off for home.

"I'll be back," I whispered—and then I heard a voice in my head saying,

"No! Your work is not here! Go back to America—why else do you think you were born there?" The 'voice' was adamant and certainly sounded a bit fed up with me. I sat up straighter.

"Your job is to write very short pieces that pack a punch! Use your ordinary life as a metaphor for the tough realities of life in the world. Tell your stories lightly and with humor, and keep them short enough to read over a cup of coffee. Make people laugh, and reassure everyone you can all make it through. Then send your pieces out to the world, and do it frequently.

Now, go home and do your job!"

So I did.

Many of them are told in this book.

I hope you've enjoyed them …

Real Magic

In early Spring, four years after Herb died, I went canoeing with a good friend in Northern Vermont—illegally, as it happened, since it was before the official opening of the season—but the air was soft and the sun warm when we set out, so we chanced it. Wendy is an experienced guide and I was her willing sidekick, so she steered in the stern and I paddled in the bow the way we'd been doing out on the water for years.

This time, however, a storm came in unexpectedly, darkening the skies and whipping the lake into huge waves, threatening to capsize us far from shore, way out of sight of where we had left the car. Oops!

Riding one breaking wave Wendy pulled a muscle in her back, so it was up to me to get us in mostly by myself, paddling like a madwoman against wild winds, following her instructions to head straight into those high waves, not to let the canoe slip sideways, while she steered with one arm!

We were both in our seventies ... How did we get here?

Okay, I figured, we would drown together in the lake's icy depths, not a bad way to go when you think about it. It wouldn't be the first time I'd tempted the Fates, but I'd made it through before, hadn't I?

And we did, thanks to Wendy steering one-handed in the stern and me powered by pure terror in the bow!

We made it across in one piece, at last scraping bottom at the far shore where we'd left the car, pulling onto a sandy beach in a slanting downpour, dumping ourselves out onto sodden ground and dragging the rain-filled canoe after us.

Bailing out with our hands to lighten the load barely made a dent, as the rain kept coming. Tipping the canoe worked not at all and trying to drag it, full of water, towards the car, was a bad joke. There was nothing to do except leave it beached and get ourselves into the car to warm up for awhile.

Once the rainburst passed we tried again, this time successfully—turning, dumping water and manhandling the heavy canoe in a single motion, and then muscling it up and over onto the roof of the car, Wendy with only one working arm!

However, on the way up I felt something snap in my midriff—heard it snap, in fact! I'd have to deal with that later—it was my price to pay. We managed to get the canoe all the way up, strap it down and get back inside, turning up the heater and stripping out of our wet clothes, shivering and laughing, rather proud of ourselves.

I was not yet in pain …

All the way home we told each other the story in hilarious detail, ready to say it all again to our friends—and my brother back at the farm—and had each other in stitches all the way back to Putney!

We had survived!

A week later in California, in the Emergency Room, I looked at my chest X-ray and couldn't miss the shadowy blob by my collarbone.

"What's that?" I asked the doctor.

"That's the problem," he replied. "It's your stomach, my friend, which does not belong there! Would you like to tell me how you did that?"

242

"You won't believe me, I swear …" I replied. He just shook his head, so I told him and thankfully, he was kind. Later, after seeing my doctor and a surgeon, it was decided I would not have the surgery but, since a displaced stomach was not necessarily life-threatening, and if I was willing to survive on smoothies, I could live with this. And they sent me home.

That evening after gagging on my smoothie, I lay disconsolate on the couch hungry and hurting, when my friend Christina dropped by. Apparently she hadn't been aware I'd been away.

"Just checking in," she said. "I had a feeling you could use some help."

"How did you know …?"

"You and I seem to do that," she replied simply. I pointed to my midriff and told her the story. She then asked, "Isn't there some kind of abdominal massage thingy … I forget what it is called …" Googling 'abdominal massage thingy' was impossible, of course, so Christina got me into PJs and bed, a smoothie by my side, sat with me for company and after awhile took her leave.

The next morning she phoned early, her voice excited.

"It's called *Chi Nei Tsang!*" She announced from the noisy hallway of the conference she was attending. "The woman sitting next to me is studying it—would you believe? Go look it up!"

Which I did. And found that there were four healers who practiced it in Berkeley, one of whom, with the wonderful name of Jak Noble, had an office right on my street! And I had never noticed. Eleven houses down, I counted. And he had one appointment open for that day!

An amazing synchronicity!

I took a seat in the Waiting Room, quite nervous, and the moment he walked in I think I stopped breathing, because I knew him! I felt I'd known him forever. He seemed to have a similar reaction to me because his eyes widened as he stopped in his tracks, staring! It was the oddest few moments, because neither of us quite knew what to do next. I had to stop myself from blurting out, "Where have you been?" and throwing my arms around him.

I think neither of us had any idea what was happening, but then the moment passed and he came forward, introducing himself and bringing me into the healing room.

I had no idea what had just happened, nor what I should do next. We both sat down awkwardly and said nothing but continued gazing. I think I mentioned that I lived up the street, then he told me about *chi nei tsang* and began reciting what sounded like Taoist poetry, but I didn't register a word. I told him I had torn my diaphragm lifting a canoe over my head in the rain, and I suspect he had no idea what I was talking about either, and neither of us quite knew what to do next. In retrospect, I would say we were both in a state of mild shock, totally incoherent and acting like a couple of idiots.

Gradually, though, we began to make sense, as if we were catching up with one another on our lives since we had last met. Whenever that was! I told him about losing my husband recently and he told me about some difficult relationships he'd had. We talked about our work and he told me that he used to be a Rock musician. Gradually we talked our way into calmer waters, and eventually I settled onto his massage table and presented my aching belly to his warm hands which, I realized from the first touch, were genius hands. I recognized the 'true heat' of a genuine healer. This man, whoever he was, could probably heal me …

We had apparently made a mysterious circle through time, but now we were right here where we needed to be, together for healing. I trusted him instinctively and simply put myself into his hands.

I wondered if each of our guardian angels were in the room with us—and if they had a sense of humor and had wondered for a long time how to maneuver us together. I imagined one saying to the other, "I have an idea …" and both bursting into angel laughter! After all, we had been neighbors on and off for years and still had not managed to meet in an ordinary way! I took a deep breath, closing my eyes and grateful for the mystery, and sensed that I had just entered a doorway into the rest of my life.

We continued meeting regularly for another two years as the explorations into my past went deeper into unknowns of this lifetime—the fears and harms, the ancestors and the descendants—and I watched his intuitive skills become sharper and more sensitive, as if we were mutual guides in this process—too old to be lovers, but grateful to have found one another again as comrades at the right moment of our lives. It felt to me like a precious gift.

"Do you understand what's going on?" I asked one day after a session in which I felt myself melting down one more level of feeling into bedrock pain. Was I ready to go there? Breathe. Release. Tears. Memories. If this were a movie, it could be called a tragicomedy. He just stood by my side quietly, one hand lightly resting on my belly, both of us breathing in tandem—then he said simply,

"Magic is real, you know."

I tell this story because of how many unplanned synchronicities had to happen for us to make our connection, go deep together, and retrieve what must have been a longtime relationship. And heal together, perhaps not for the first time.

It was metaphoric, and we ourselves were the metaphor as every human dilemma is a metaphor of this changing world of ours! Just now, as the world goes through paroxysms literal and symbolic, volcanoes are erupting on islands in the oceans, pouring out hot magma and creating new land in the process. Oceans are responding with tidal waves, and wildlife is figuring out new ways of surviving. We humans, stuck indoors in a pandemic are dreaming up new ways of living, and teaching that to our children even as we discover deeper parts of ourselves and new ways of learning about the world and about the nature of reality.

These are the times we live in, like it or not, even if it strains our abilities to respond: even if the climate changes radically and pandemics take us by storm; even when our financial systems prove they support only the very few, and the environment not at all.

Even when we are terrified of everything from death and taxes to one another; even if we feel unloved and lonely and the oceans are polluted with plastics and the whales are hunted down mercilessly … even if the era we are living in comes to an end and living beings die back into the earth for an era of rest until it is Time to start up again, slowly, miraculously, newly born—hopefully wiser than we are now—it probably would not be happening for the first time.

We have been here and done this before—more than once, I wager.

Even if you and I are on the planet right now on purpose, to help make this difficult transition to the next phase of our history on earth, having been through this before at another time and from another place, finding one another, who knows where or how, learning that our hearts can think at least as well as our brains and our dreams are at least as real as the bus waiting down at the corner.

For help, apparently, is closer than we think and it seems to be right down the street; it has probably been there for years without our knowing, even if it takes a severe shock to wake us up and take notice that we are in this life together, no matter what, and sometimes we have to come close to death before we take notice and find one another in the storm.

In the magic which, as Jak and I now know, is real.

Saving Grace

for Nassim Haramein and Gregg Braden

These past weeks I have been taking an online course in the new Science with the geologist Gregg Braden and the physicist Nassim Haramein who, for the past 30 years, have been working together to understand Einstein's predictions on the Unified Field now that recent Mathematical formulas were there to support his theories.

They have apparently succeeded in proving, through the rules of basic physics, that the universe is a unified Whole on all levels and dimensions, interconnected through Time and Space and beyond, cycling through universal patterns, emerging into form and dissolving back into the matrix endlessly.

Unified at every level.

I was very excited to learn about these fellows, because I always had a soft spot for Professor Einstein whose ideas, even though I couldn't follow his mathematics, struck a deep chord with me. I mostly felt like an undercover agent for his conclusions, because I intuitively understood what he was reaching for—although to me it felt more like Poetry than Math. I 'sensed' it rather than 'thought' it, and used it in my own ways to make Art.

I have spent my life tracking it down the way a cat stalks a mouse through tall grasses; first here, then there, sniffing and feeling my way, pouncing and batting things around, glancing away, then waiting …

Initially I looked to religion; first, the Judaism I was born into, then Medieval Christianity in France, then singing Gospel in a Black church; as a dancer I studied the body in motion, feeling how I mirrored the ongoing cycling of the Universe. In India, as a medic, I observed birth and death up close, and on an uninhabited island in the Galápagos I lived alone for a week with sea lions and ocean-feeding reptiles, diving seabirds by the thousands and a night sky thick with stars and galaxies, arrayed endlessly above me, where I was but a tiny dot on the planet.

I wanted to see what Charles Darwin had seen, and it took my breath away.

I took on hunger issues in the community, and I sat by the bedsides of men dying of AIDS, always watching for clues of the 'bigger picture'—and my most profound lessons were learned as a wife and mother with my husband and our three children, continuing to search for the glue that bound it, and us, all together.

I have read somewhere that the intuitive way of knowing things in their Wholeness has to be 'caught' rather than 'taught.' I believe that, because I tend to 'feel' the truth of things, rather than 'think' them, as my insights have a way of catching me by surprise and revealing, by sensory clues, what I had been searching for with my mind. In any case, I believe it was developing this ability to feel my way towards 'knowing' that got me through a desperate childhood at a hard time in the world.

I am so thankful I have lived to witness my intuitive understandings of the world presented in scientific language by, as they are called, the 'peer-reviewed' scientists Nassim Haramein and Gregg Braden, one a physicist and the other a geologist. They have worked together quietly for 30 years, thinking outside the box and seeking answers not only in their respective disciplines, but in archeology and ancient history and art as well, finding all of it relevant to their quest.

I pray it is not too late for enough of us—only 51% of us are needed, I am told—to turn this ship around in mid-ocean and head for a new shore; an ocean that is teeming with deadly particles of plastic thanks to the Polymer Chemists who neglected to ask what would happen to this marvelous invention after the 'plastic bags and bottles' were used by us?

Sorry to rant, but I've had to watch this happen while keeping my mouth shut …

The fact is, I love science, and once thought to become a Geologist. I married a scientist and gave birth to scientists and continue to long for them all to integrate the way Science perceives our world with the way intuitives and artists perceive the world—in a both/and way. We live in the same world, after all, and though we may experience the world through different lenses, that does not mean one 'side' is right, and the other 'wrong.' Like the blind men and the elephant, there are so many ways of looking! We are all correct—we just have to put our perspectives together to get at the truth!

It's not so hard to do—really!

Nassim and Gregg hopefully have made a way through; I believe they have, and the moment of truth may be NOW! If not, I fear it could be curtains for everyone—pink iguanas and manatees, ancient forests and mountain thyme, all of it!

And us.

"How do you know?" I have been asked. "What's your proof?" I've been dismissed by teachers and family, disbelieved by polite friends and now, facing the inevitable crises of our environment and the run-away economy, and the fear … the fear … of not only Death, but of Life itself, it is time to speak up.

For Professor Einstein, if not for you and me. Here, in essence, is what I believe a growing number of scientists and poets, children (have you noticed?) and indigenous elders are saying:

Everything is interconnected, and the pattern of the whole Universe is mirrored in the physical world at every level. Fractals. As above, so below.

The basis of all being is Consciousness, which underlies All Things and is not just a product of the human brain.

Everything cycles at every level, in every dimension of what we call 'incarnation' and appears, grows, ages and slips back into the Whole from which it came, but never disappears. What we call Death is simply a stage in the endless process of Life unfolding.

There is nothing to fear because every one of us is an intrinsic part of the Whole, and remain so in the Consciousness that encompasses both Time and Space. We remain connected to the Whole of Creation by a force of attraction that we humans experience as Love—but a Love so profound we mostly cannot begin to understand it in our human state—except, perhaps in that magical time of falling madly in love ...

We're here to figure this all out, I believe, and to reach a state of personal clarity such that we love ourselves quite well, thank you very much, and therefore can love one another as well, and when it comes time to ride the wave back into the toroidal Whole, through what we call 'Death,' we can hug one another and share a last laugh together before melting back into the whole sweet wave, blowing kisses as we go.

Again ... and again ... and again ...

I bid Thee farewell until we meet again next time, and then the next ... somewhere out there/in here in the Cosmos ...

Loving Franco

I was 20 when I left home for my first adventure abroad, and brought with me a backpack containing only one change of clothes, a poncho for rain, sandals for sun, a journal to write in, and my flute. With a scholarship to study Medieval Art History awaiting me in France, I had three whole months to wander before the school term started, so I was free to take to the road and have my adventures before I had to settle down and study the Middle Ages.

As it happened, I found I was good at getting lost. I would start out for one place but find myself, either by mistake or last minute whim, somewhere else—like when I bought a bus ticket for Chartres and ended up in the tiny village of Chars, near Reims, where I had a memorable overnight adventure with the good people of Chars. Mostly, I made it a game, for this was my maiden voyage and the world was, as they say, my oyster and if I had been less ditsy I would never have met Franco on a train in Italy, headed for the coast. I had bought a ticket for Florence but had boarded on the wrong platform and taken the train going to Ravenna instead. In the opposite direction. Ooops...

Oh well, all was not lost as Ravenna has many 12th century churches—with mosaics!—so I looked in my guidebook, noted there was a youth hostel in Ravenna, and settled down for my first real adventure in Europe.

At Bologna, a group of musicians came on and noisily scrambled for seats—except for one fellow with a cello case who stepped onto the train, stood his cello beside him and reached for a hanging strap. He was neither tall nor strikingly handsome, but still I could hardly take my eyes off him. He had the unusual quality of simply belonging where he was, at ease in his body, and I tried not to stare as the train picked up speed. He seemed to ride its jagged rhythms like a surfer riding a wave, the way a dancer might move easily across a stage, and when he smiled to one of his friends and I heard the velvety timbre of his voice, I paid attention.

I casually let my flute case poke out of my backpack to signal to him, should he look, that I was also a musician.

One by one, the others left the train as we crossed the countryside of Emilia until he and I were the only ones left in the car. Moving to one of the vacated seats, he sat down onto one facing me and smiled from across the aisle. I smiled back, then lowered my head and paged again through the guide book, memorizing the address of the youth hostel—or pretended to, suddenly feeling very shy. When we both got off at the last stop he approached me on the platform, hoisting his cello into one arm.

"I saw you looking for the youth hostel on your map of Ravenna," he commented in careful Italian. I replied, in an awkward patois of mostly French with some Italian words and he shifted to his own patois of mostly Italian with some French words. From the very beginning, we spoke our own private language.

"I live right across from the *Ostello*, so we can go together," he said, pointing to a waiting tram outside the station, which we boarded and as the tram clattered through the streets of Ravenna I learned that he played with the Bologna Opera Orchestra and was practicing to audition for the Maggio Musicale in the Fall, and he learned that I was American, would be going to school in France for the year and was learning to play the flute. It was easy to talk to him—even in a made-up language—and we both smiled a lot as we exchanged bits of information about ourselves, though I doubt that any of this would have become the story it became, if the youth hostel had not already been full when we got there.

"I forgot to mention that it is always filled by this time of day," he told me with a grin. "So I guess you have no choice but to stay with me." When I felt myself blushing crimson, he corrected himself, "no, no with my family, *mi madre e papa e mes deux soeurs...*" he quickly assured me.

"But I am just a stranger that you met on a train!" I insisted.

"And are we not *les compagnions de la musica?* So we are not strangers," he insisted back.

With my heart in my throat, I nodded and took a deep breath, following him through the door and up the two flights of stairs to their apartment, wondering if I were at last starting to live my true life and if this was how magic actually happened in the real world when nobody was watching you.

"For just this night," I said cautiously. He just smiled.

A week later I was still there with his excitable, welcoming family, almost like a third sister to the girls, who were already planning my wedding with their brother in San Vitale—by next year, they told me—and designing my elaborate wedding veil.

By day, while he practiced at home for his auditions, I found my way to the mosaic-filled churches around the city, astonished by their brilliance, one after another. He would only practice when I was out of the house, and when I asked when I might hear him play he smiled mysteriously and said that *claro*, I could not leave them until I had heard him play, so he was in no a hurry to play for me. What could I say?

In fact, it took another week before I heard him play his cello because he left for a short tour with the Orchestra while Mama and I got onto a bus for their tiny village in the hills the family had come from, and I got to meet his excitable extended family, unable to understand a word of their dialect! But they patted me and we smiled a lot, and Mama told them all about how Franco had brought me home with him, nary a word of which I could follow.

Finally, when Mama and I and Franco all arrived home in Ravenna, Mama and I laden with mushrooms from the hills, eggs from the hens, and marinated cherries in jars, he offered to play for us after supper.

In the center of his bedroom he set up his chair, music stand and cello. Mama stood by the door in her apron, flushed with excitement and a wooden spoon in her flour-smeared hand. Papa took his chair by the window, hands tucked into his armpits, and the girls were downstairs visiting the neighbors. I was invited to make myself comfortable on his bed and sat down carefully, my legs tucked under me. Then he sat, picked up bow and cello and closed his eyes.

The first notes were like breaths of air, felt more than heard. He was stroking the cello into life with a quiet melody line and every vibration of the strings seemed to enter my body like light-tipped arrows. I could barely breathe. When the music rose into rich melody I felt the whole room shake, as if I were a resonating chamber for the sounds. I wanted to sing along with it, to cry out loud. I felt like fainting into his pillow. I had never heard music like this before!

By the end of the piece Babbo and I were both in tears. Franco, head down, just sat there, his bow lifted until the sounds had quieted from the air of the room and then Mama thwacked the doorpost with her wooden spoon, shouting Bravo!

I was speechless.

"*Ti piache?*" Franco asked me quietly. Did you like it?...All I could do was nod and stare. And breathe in the fragrance of him on his pillow. "*Molto...*" I finally whispered, trembling.

I had no idea the cello could sound so emotional, so passionate, so like a human voice.

Who was this quiet fellow, intense and … foreign? How had we managed to find one another out there in the whole wide world—on a train? How had I been led here, to these gentle people with their brilliant son—what made me take that 'wrong' train?

I wonder if we had to meet—sometime in this life—to know love with one another. Franco had my heart—probably from the moment I watched him board the train in Bologna—although perhaps not to marry, as his sisters wished to believe.

If we had, however, I believe we would have chosen to have the wedding at Sant Appolinare-in-Classe, the 5th century Basilica now several kilometers inland from the coast, and not at San Vitale. Classe was where we had first declared our love, and the miracle of our meeting, and it is where we performed together the next Christmas Eve at the Midnight Mass, when I returned to Ravenna from France—taking the correct train, this time—to share the holidays with the family.

Actually, we played there twice, both surprise gifts from Franco who told me that the Padre was his friend, and we had gotten permission to play in the Basilica the day before Christmas. It was his gift to me, he told me, but then he secretly had my flute brought to the Mass with the family the next night and, with an impish smile he handed it to me saying, "That was a rehearsal, *mia cara*, this is the performance."

If I may say so myself, that may have been the most sensual musical celebration of the Mass ever heard at that altar in centuries—if ever!

It was also where we came to understand, finally, that we could not marry. Our lives were too different. I probably could never be happy as an Italian housewife of that era, my entire focus on husband and children. I was a questioner, always wondering about spirit and consciousness and fascinated by subjects like Medieval Church history! (My fiancé back home—yes, I had one and yes, he was a scholar—called me and himself "eggheads.")

Franco and I finally had our hard conversation that night, well past midnight on Christmas Eve after the others all had returned to Ravenna, beneath the mosaic cupola where we had just played like angels up into its resonant spaces celebrating, with his community, the birth of a savior God on the Winter Solstice. We declared our love and we cried. Then we laughed and both shook our heads, No.

Chokingly he confessed that he was already engaged to be married and I, relieved, confessed that I was too, and there in the darkened sanctuary we burst into teary laughter and embraced hard, weeping in one another's arms.

We parted on the first day of the New Year in Venice, after spending our last few days together there, and through the years we have never lost touch.

We each married our promised partners—in the same year on different sides of the ocean—sending wedding gifts and photos of the children at regular intervals. In one of my books, I wrote our story, but since he did not read English, I doubt that he ever saw it.

His son followed him in the cello section of the Maggio Musicale, and last week it was through this son—who has the same name as my oldest son—that I learned of Franco's death.

This story is my way of remembering and honoring him. Loving him again.

It is the end of an era, although not the end of a love affair. I expect we shall meet again as the deep friends the world meant us to be, by putting me on the right platform this time so that we find one another again as we travel on through the ethers.

Ciao Franco!

I am now also approaching my own platform, my own life track headed to the next stop which, I believe, is not a stop at all, but an opening to an infinite place that I will recognize as Home.

We will meet there, Franco and I. I wonder if he and Herb have met up there yet? I wonder if they ever think of me...?

Death happens, and it is okay. Just as birth happens and the cycle makes its circuits—so does death happen

to Herb

to Franco

to you

to me...

CAROLYN NORTH

www.ingramcontent.com/pod-product-compliance
Lightning Source LLC
Chambersburg PA
CBHW052034090426
42739CB00010B/1904